D0849757

WHITE EVANGELICAL RACISM

WHITE EVANGELICAL RACISM

The Politics of Morality in America

ANTHEA BUTLER

ᒥᒣ

A Ferris and Ferris Book

THE UNIVERSITY OF NORTH CAROLINA PRESS

Chapel Hill

This book was published under the
Marcie Cohen Ferris and William R. Ferris Imprint
of the University of North Carolina Press.

Manufactured in the United States of America
Designed and set in Miller and DIN types by Kim Bryant
The University of North Carolina Press has been a member
of the Green Press Initiative since 2003.

Cover illustration: background © iStock.com/kyoshino;
flag © iStock.com/GoodLifeStudio

Library of Congress Cataloging-in-Publication Data
Names: Butler, Anthea D., 1960– author.
Title: White evangelical racism : the politics of morality in
America / Anthea Butler.
Description: Chapel Hill : The University of North Carolina
Press, [2021] | "A Ferris and Ferris book." |
Includes bibliographical references and index.
Identifiers: LCCN 2020047941 | ISBN 9781469661179 (cloth) |
ISBN 9781469661186 (ebook)
Subjects: LCSH: Evangelicalism—United States—History. |
Racism—Religious aspects—Christianity. | Christians, White—
United States—History. | Religion and politics—United States—
History. | Racism—United States—History. | United States—
Church history. | United States—Race relations.
Classification: LCC BR563.W45 B88 2021 | DDC
305.6/80408900973—dc23
LC record available at https://lccn.loc.gov/2020047941

For
Bill Pannell
&
Walter
Hollenweger

Thank you
for
lighting
the
antiracism
path

CONTENTS

WHITE EVANGELICAL RACISM

INTRODUCTION

Evangelical Racism: A Feature, Not a Bug

White Evangelical Racism tells a concise history of the evangelical movement and—here is the hard part—the racist and racial elements that imbue its beliefs, practices, and social and political activism. It is racism that binds and blinds many white American evangelicals to the vilification of Muslims, Latinos, and African Americans. It is racism that impels many evangelicals to oppose immigration and turn a blind eye to children in cages at the border. It is racism that fuels evangelical Islamophobia. It was evangelical acceptance of biblically sanctioned racism that motivated believers to separate and sell families during slavery and to march with the Klan. Racist evangelicals shielded cross burners, protected church burners, and participated in lynchings. Racism is a feature, not a bug, of American evangelicalism.

I will take you onto the third rail of American religious history, focusing on the key issues evangelicals have succeeded in shaping—especially those that have influenced our current politics. Starting with the slaveholding Christianity of Frederick Douglass's era, this history bridges, as did Douglass's life, slavery and emancipation. It churns through the eras of Reconstruction, Jim Crow, and relentless violence. It leans deeply into the rise of Billy Graham and the civil rights era, arriving at birtherism and the rise of the man some evangelicals refer to as King Cyrus, Donald Trump. It looks from there into the future. It looks directly at the choice white evangelicals must make if they can justly perceive the history of racism embedded in their tradition: Will they allow racism to continue to taint their faith, or will they reject it?

I can invert the story, too: this book is a short primer on the history of racism as directly implicated in conveying the vast majority of white evangelicals to their unabashed embrace of contemporary right-wing politics. To be clear, not all white evangelicals embrace the kind of conservative politics that build on the foundation of racism. Today, a small but growing number of white evangelicals belong to churches and movements that robustly evangelical allegiances aligned with political activity, namely that of the Republican Party. While it is true that one could look at Black evangelicals like Tom Skinner and others, their political leanings did not align with those of the majority of white evangelicals, who embraced the Republican Party starting in the 1970s. The ubiquitous support demonstrated by white evangelicals for the Republican Party made them not just religiously or culturally white: it made them politically white conservatives in America concerned with keeping the status quo of patriarchy, cultural hegemony, and nationalism.

White evangelicals' stark identification with the Republican Party also became a handy catchall for pollsters eager to measure evangelicals' impact politically. Many historians of evangelicalism, such as Mark Noll, Thomas Kidd, David Bebbington, and George Marsden, have been concerned for much of their academic careers with defining evangelicalism via theology and history. Their projects are not expressly concerned with racial, nationalistic, and political concerns of conservative white Americans. Evangelicals are, however, concerned with their political alliance with the Republican Party and with maintaining the cultural and racial whiteness that they have transmitted to the public. This is the working definition of American evangelicalism. American print and television media have embraced and promoted this definition, and the American public has accepted it. So for the purposes of this book, the word "evangelical," unless otherwise noted, should be read as WHITE evangelical.

"To a great extent, the evangelical church in America supported the status quo. It supported slavery; it supported segregation; it preached against any attempt of the black man to stand on his own two feet." These words, uttered in 1970 by Tom Skinner—the son of a Black preacher and a former gang member turned evangelist—still ring true today. In an impassioned speech titled "Racism and World Evangelicalism," given at the Inter-Varsity Christian Fellowship's Urbana conference, Skinner challenged the large crowd of young white Christians to look more closely at the history of evangelical complicity in racism in America. For the very small number of Black evangelicals who were present, it was a promising moment in which Skinner affirmed their experiences with racism in the evangelical movement.

Skinner's claim that evangelicalism supported the status quo, slavery, and segregation is not hyperbole. It speaks to a history that is obscured by some historians of evangelicalism who cannot or will not deal with the racism at the core of evangelical beliefs, practices, and political allegiances— with good reason. Evangelicals today are not only a religious group but also a powerful voting bloc of Republicans and a strong lobby on Capitol Hill. They have their own colleges, universities, and secondary education facilities. They are embedded in local and state governments all over the United States. They have been loyal Republican voters since the late 1970s. In the 2016 election, 81 percent of evangelical voters supported Donald Trump, and this support continues to hold firm now. Yet many political commentators seem stymied by evangelicals' love for Trumpism. There are many reasons for this love, but one reason is most important: racism. Evangelicals' support for current-day policies that seem draconian and unchristian is linked inescapably to a foundational history that we will uncover in this book. American history chronicles evangelical support for and participation in racist structures in America. Skinner got it right.

We will look at how nineteenth-century Bible reading helped pave the path that took us to 2016 and into the present. Hundreds of articles and a fair number of books have been written in attempts to understand evangelicals' rock-solid support for Trumpism. John Fea came up with a name for the large number of evangelicals who surround Trump: "court evangelicals." These are the evangelicals who obtained virtually unrestricted access to Trump's White House, where they prayed for him regularly and advised him triumphantly on matters large and small.

It was the lament of some evangelicals, however, that gave me pause. One important lament was expressed in Michael Gerson's poignant article "The Last Temptation," published in the *Atlantic* in

Gerson's misty-eyed longing for a virtuous evangelical heyday conveniently leaves too many events out of the historical narrative. For instance, let us look at a narrative that embraces historical knowledge about how people read the Bible in the nineteenth century. We know that biblical beliefs about slavery were embedded in the theologies of Baptists and Presbyterians. The supposed inferiority of enslaved Africans rested on biblical interpretations of the stories of Adam and Eve and Noah. For many white Protestants, the Bible pointed to an inferiority and a subhuman quality of enslaved Africans. Predestination—the Calvinist theology stating that God chose some to be predestined for salvation before their birth—not only was part of the culture and religion of slaveholders but would later become the foundation of the apartheid movement in South Africa. These are important biblical beliefs that evangelicals embraced and continued to perpetuate long after the Emancipation Proclamation. From using the Bible to support slavery to opposing the civil rights movement, integration, and interracial marriage, evangelicals have long employed a presumed moral authority to hide their prejudices.

Today, these biblical prohibitions show up in interesting ways. In the summer of 2019 in Mississippi, a couple was turned down when trying to rent Boone's Camp Event Hall for their wedding reception. Why? The couple, a Black man and white woman, was told by the event hall owner, "First of all, we don't do gay weddings or mixed race . . . because of our Christian race, I mean, our Christian belief." The hall owner's slip of the tongue was telling in its equation of Christianity with whiteness. For evangelicals, "Christian race," America, and belief are synonymous. Christianity is whiteness as well as belief. It is this conflation that causes evangelicals to ignore their racism. They truly believe that their Christianity is a race, and this comprises an all-encompassing identity. That is why when some evangelicals say they don't see color, they really mean it. They just see whiteness. No color but the dominant one.

For many white evangelicals reading my words, this will be a hard truth to swallow. After all, you may have been taught that evangelicals were abolitionists, supported the poor, did mission work around the globe, and made a better world for everyone. And clearly, many did.

But many also supported slavery, split churches, believed African Americans were inferior to whites, supported Jim Crow, and avidly opposed civil rights, busing, and interracial marriage. Many harassed gays, called AIDS a curse from God, and vilified Muslims after 9/11. So when evangelical writers claim that they do not understand the overwhelming nature of evangelical support for rightwing and sometimes downright scurrilous Republican candidates and politicos, they fail to reckon with evangelical history.

Evangelicals are not naïve individuals who were taken advantage of by a slick New York real estate mogul and reality TV star. They were his accomplices. Their prayers and shows of piety surrounding conservative elected officials—most notably in recent times, the forty-fifth president—are a feature, not a bug, of nineteenth- and twentieth-century American evangelicalism. Race and racism have always been foundational parts of evangelicalism in America, fueling its educational, political, social, and cultural mores.

Evangelicals occupy an important place in the story of American religion—but they also are key to our nation's politics of now. The set of evangelicals who believed in and continue today to believe in the inferiority of people of color are complicit in supporting structures of oppression that are antithetical to the gospel they claim to believe in. Further, their claims of virtue surrounding sexuality, family, money, and limited government fall short in the face of their leaders' foibles. One only has to remember Jimmy Swaggart crying "I have sinned" after being caught soliciting prostitutes in the 1980s or Ted Haggard, former president of the National Association of Evangelicals, being caught having a sexual relationship with a man after he had berated gays in the documentary *Jesus Camp*. But because conservative evangelicalism embraces patriarchal culture imbued with a persecution complex, its leaders will always have an excuse for their excesses, transgressions, and sins. And sin for evangelicals is always personal, not corporate, and God is always available to forgive deserving individuals, especially, it seems, if the sinner is a white man. The sin of racism, too, can be swept away with an event or a confession. Rarely do evangelicals admit to a need for restitution.

I have taught and written about American evangelicalism for the past twenty years, and questions about the movement have always haunted me: Does being evangelical really mean being white? Does it mean that anyone who embraces evangelical beliefs has to give up parts of their culture? Does it mean that evangelicals always have to vote Republican?

To be honest, I have always known the answers. Evangelicalism is synonymous with whiteness. It is not only a cultural whiteness but also a political whiteness. The presupposition of the whiteness of evangelicalism has come to define evangelicalism, and it is the definition that the media, the general public, and politicians agree on.

As a former evangelical—yes, it's true—who continues to have friends in the tradition, I am at times sympathetic to the distorted position in which my friends find themselves. Yet I am tired of the shenanigans. Evangelicals who are embarrassed by the worship of Trumpism have twisted themselves into knots to claim a kinship with evangelicals of color in order to avoid being judged as right-wingers. Others are leaving the fold altogether, as Robert Jones points out in his prescient book *The End of White Christian America*. Still others lament evangelical voting patterns but remain in the fold due to their commitments to scripture, the pro-life movement, and opposition to same-sex marriage. The hard truth is that evangelicals are one of the most, if not the most, polarizing voting groups in America, and the racism, sexism, and patriarchal structure of their movement has embedded itself within the Republican Party.

As a *political* movement, evangelicalism wields enormous power despite its declining numbers. As such, evangelical history, and especially its racist history, must be scrutinized in order to truly understand the movement's political, social, and moral stances in the twenty-first century. "It is the strangest story: how so many evangelicals lost their interest in decency, and how a religious tradition called by grace became defined by resentment," writes Michael Gerson.

Racism is the key to this strange story. Because of racism, evangelical decency was lost, and evangelicals' resentments grew. This book aims to tell the story evangelicals won't.

American Christian rapper Lecrae. While discussing racism in a conversation that was a bit too rosy in tone, Giglio tried to explain how white privilege works. Instead, speaking the words that open this chapter, he inadvertently attested to a sentiment held dear by many Christians who lived in the nineteenth century.

Giglio's "we miss the blessing of slavery" in fact, echoed the lines from George Fitzhugh's 1857 proslavery book *Cannibals All! or, Slaves without Masters*. Though more than a century and a half divide Fitzhugh from Giglio, both men understood one bald truth: slavery was a blessing to white people and a curse to Black people. Giglio's comments caused such an outcry that he posted a video apology on social media the very next day. His explanation was that he had been trying to get people to understand the meaning of the term "white privilege" and that—using inappropriate words—he had done a bad job of it. While Giglio dealt with the ensuing social media meltdown and public relations debacle, it was Lecrae who ended up suffering the most criticism from African American Christians, who chided him for missing the on-air moment when he could have offered a timely and potent corrective to Giglio's statement. Black Christians saw in that minute the power of white evangelicalism to reduce Lecrae, even though he had tried to gently object, to a nodding prop for the white evangelical pastor. The discussion showed how Giglio, though attempting to talk openly about race, had nonetheless structured the whole meeting in a way that placed the Black man in a position subordinate to Giglio's religious authority.

I begin with this painful story because it says so much about both the continuity between evangelicalism and slavery and the connection between the evangelical movements of the antebellum era and of today. It reveals that racism was structured— with the exact same words Pastor Giglio used—into American evangelicalism across the centuries.

Slavery is the foundation of racism and power in American evangelicalism. Responses to slavery, both for and against, have fundamentally shaped the evangelical movement in a number of important ways. Many insightful works of history have been written helping to uncover and comb out this story. Drawing on them, this chapter builds out the essential foundation of the story in order to navigate the early period as an introduction to the twentieth- and twenty-first-century history of evangelical racism that will form the rest of this book.

As a historian, I know that American evangelicals made important and substantial contributions to the abolitionist movement and to the education and uplift of African Americans during Reconstruction. I am deliberately focusing this chapter on the trajectory of evangelical history that supported slavery, the Lost Cause, Jim Crow, and lynching. My reason for shaping this book around that trajectory—which I have no doubt is extremely painful to both Black and most white evangelicals today—is that this history is the key to understanding how evangelicals used and continue to use scripture, morality, and the political power they gathered across the course of the twentieth and, now, the twenty-first centuries.

The nineteenth-century racism of American evangelicalism shored up southern cultural and racial mores through the interpretation of scriptures, theology, and belief that informed white southerners' social and political actions. Evangelicals' use of morality in the nineteenth century forged the pathway by which racism and white supremacy became part and parcel of evangelical history, informing how they interpreted scripture, how they constructed a public and nationalistic vision for America, and how they used morality to both convert and oppress African Americans in slavery and in freedom.

To understand how evangelicals went about this process, we must begin with the Bible, because the Bible was the defining text to which people turned to answer the question of whether slavery was or was not God's will. Before the Civil War, the Bible was interpreted literally, and most people's acquaintance with it came through their pastor or, if they happened to be people of means, through their own copy (most likely sold to them by an agent of the American Bible Society). Although many did not have a Bible in their own homes, they heard scripture often enough in their churches to acquire a familiarity and could quote their favorite verses by heart. Some scriptures, however, were often repeated in order to support slavery.

The two most cited biblical scriptures used to support nineteenth-century slavery in the United States were Genesis 9:18–27 and Ephesians 6:5–7. One was an admonition, the other a justification for why people of African descent were to be enslaved. Genesis 9:18–27 tells the story of Noah and his three sons, Shem, Ham, and Japheth. When Noah got drunk and fell asleep naked, his son Ham saw his nakedness. He told his brothers, Shem and Japheth, who entered the tent where Noah was sleeping but walked in backward so they would not see their father's nakedness. Once there, they covered their father to preserve his dignity. When Noah awakened and realized what had happened, he cursed Ham, the father of Canaan: "Cursed be Canaan; a servant of servants shall he be unto his brethren. And he said, Blessed be the Lord God of Shem; and Canaan shall be his servant. God shall enlarge Japheth, and he shall dwell in the tents of Shem; and Canaan shall be his servant." Nineteenth-century expositors generally regarded "Canaan" as Africa and interpreted Ham as representing Black peoples. They concluded that Noah's curse relegated Black peoples to chattel slavery. The name "Ham" was interpreted erroneously to mean "dark" or "black." This scripture became the foundation of the biblical justification for slavery for many southern slaveholders in the United States as well as for northerners who supported slavery.

Ephesians 6:5–7 offered slaveholders an even more compelling argument. It reads: "Servants, be obedient to them that are your masters according to the flesh, with fear and trembling, in singleness of your heart, as unto Christ; not with eye-service, as men-pleasers; but as the servants of Christ, doing the will of God from the heart; with good will doing service, as to the Lord, and not to men: knowing that whatsoever good thing any man doeth, the same shall he receive of the Lord, whether he be bond or free." This passage was interpreted to mean that slaves should remain docile and obey their masters, as God required of them. In the literal understanding of this scripture, it was God's will that they were slaves and therefore nothing could be done about it.

These scriptures, along with others, were used by both preachers and slaveholders to reinforce the right to hold slaves. There was even a slave Bible produced in England that omitted passages about freedom, which was used in the Caribbean by slaves who could read. Since reading was prohibited for slaves in the United States, preachers simply omitted talking about scriptures that emphasized freedom. Enslaved Africans were often told that Genesis 9:18–27 and Ephesians 6:5–7, along with other biblical scriptures, justified and explained their status as slaves. They were reminded to be obedient and in return were promised heaven, where they would be able to "serve" their eternal masters.

The Bible gave southern evangelical slaveholders a code for personal behavior that was steeped in moral practices that allowed them to define themselves as moral actors. The rationale went like this: slavery was a sin, but if a *Christian* owner held slaves, the Christian was not sinful, because God had ordained slavery in the Bible. Thomas R. Dew, slaveholder and president of the College of William and Mary, made his proslavery arguments to the Virginia legislature in the wake of the Nat Turner rebellion in Virginia along these same lines: "With regard to the assertion, that slavery is against the spirit of Christianity, we are ready to admit the general assertion, but deny most positively that there is anything in the Old or New Testament, which would go to show that slavery, when once introduced, ought at all events to be abrogated, or that the master commits any offence in holding slaves. The children of Israel themselves were slave holders, and were not condemned for it." This line of thinking was common to slaveholders. Yes, slavery was generally condemned in the scriptures, but it was allowed; no one in scripture put a stop to it, and therefore it definitely was permissible. Dew also challenged Thomas Jefferson's assertion that to as "hush arbors," to preach and practice Christianity, as well as traditional African religions, away from their masters and overseers. Interpreting stories of the Israelites fleeing Egypt and of Moses as the deliverer in terms of their own lives and stories, slaves sang songs and engaged in coded practices that turned the meaning of scriptures into cloaked messages of hope. No matter what was preached to them, slaves' religion was about freedom, both here on earth and in the hereafter. The enslaved knew that the Christianity taught to them was not the only version, and they expressed their secret knowledge through songs, signals, and words that whites did not understand, which held hidden meanings about freedom.

Slaves and free Black Americans brought this understanding of the Christian message to explicitly criticize southern evangelicalism as well. One of the strongest critiques of slaveholding Christianity in the nineteenth century is in Frederick Douglass's 1845 autobiography, *Narrative of the Life of Frederick Douglass*. For Douglass, slaveholding Christianity had no relationship to true Christianity. "Between the Christianity of this land, and the Christianity of Christ," he wrote, "I recognize the widest possible difference." Douglass told the story of a Reverend Weeden who lived near his master and who beat a female slave mercilessly, keeping her back raw for weeks. Of Weeden, Douglass said, "For all the slaveholders I have ever met, religious slaveholders are the worst. I have ever found them to be the meanest, and basest, the most cruel and cowardly, of all others." In a poem that closed his biography, Douglass described Christian slaveholders as hypocrites:

> We wonder how such saints can sing,
> Or praise the Lord upon the wing,
> Who roar, and scold, and whip, and sting,
> And to their slaves and mammon cling,
> In guilty conscience union.

Douglass, of course, provided fuel for the abolitionist movement, in which white evangelicals also participated. Abolitionists' critiques of slavery in broadsides, newspapers like the *North Star* and the *Liberator*, and books like *Uncle Tom's Cabin* became touch points in the antislavery movement, challenging the moral structure of religious slaveholding.

Moreover, debates over scripture and slavery among evangelicals divided denominations. The Methodists, Presbyterians, and Baptists all split over slavery before the Civil War. The Methodist Episcopal Church split in 1844 because one of its bishops, J. O. Andrew, acquired slaves through marriage. When Andrew was asked to step down from his post, southern delegates drafted a plan of separation. The next year, they left and formed the Methodist Episcopal Church, South. The American

Baptist denomination split the following year over opposition to appointing slaveholders as missionaries and created what we now know as the Southern Baptist Convention. Presbyterians endured several splits, the third of which, in 1861, was primarily about slavery. These differences over slavery would last into the twentieth and even the twenty-first century: the American Baptists and the Southern Baptist Convention still exist as separate entities.

Churches remained true to the social structures of the regions they lived in, and their leaders found scriptures to buttress those social structures. Biblical mandates were found to support the system of slavery, including the economics of the practice, and to be a repository for a morality constructed on the dubious value of slaveholding and southern morals as a marker of "true civilization." That civilization would be upheld after the Civil War through violence and allegiance to what historian Charles Reagan Wilson called the "Religion of the Lost Cause."

The Religion of the Lost Cause blended Christian and southern values of slaveholding. Ministers in the South believed that their former way of life, and their former society, was key to Christian civilization. The end of the Civil War did not mark the end of this particular belief. Pushing back against the destruction of their way of life, minsters deployed various methods to maintain the religious and cultural values of the slaveholding South during the Reconstruction period. Wilson notes that ministers promoted the link to these values by creating ritualistic forms that celebrated regional and mythological beliefs. By creating a history where the brutality and suffering of Black people was ignored in favor of promoting southern life and chivalry, the Lost Cause essentially turned the states of the former Confederacy into defenders of a noble ideal rather than just violent secessionists that had defied the Union.

Ministers used the mythology of the Lost Cause to promote moral reform, conversion to Christianity, and the education of the young in southern traditions. In the process, they recast the Confederacy as a defense not of slavery but of the South, its traditions, and the superiority of the southern way of life as a moral exemplar against the North. This Lost Cause aesthetic, according to historian W. Scott Poole, was steeped in romanticism and evangelicalism, and it replaced slavery as the cohesive narrative of the South. It also maintained the most important element of slavery: the idea that Black people were inferior to whites and therefore unable to take an equal place economically or socially in the Reconstruction South. All of this reinforced the boundaries of racial identity, reaffirmed antebellum attitudes regarding gender, and fueled a revivified Confederate nationalism.

The Lost Cause was buttressed by cultural behaviors steeped in religious practices and moral beliefs. Mourning the Confederate dead, erecting public statuary to Confederate generals, and creating holidays all turned the Lost Cause into a civil religion that was supported by the clergy. The birthday of Jefferson Davis, president of the Confederacy, for example, was used as the date for the establishment of Confederate Memorial Day, begun in 1866 by the Ladies' Memorial Association of Columbus, Georgia. In preserving the rituals and customs of the South and the Confederacy through the Daughters of the Confederacy and other societies, white women played an important role in cementing the structures of morality and civility that were also part of evangelical belief.

White southern women were not mere bystanders. They came to serve as an important cornerstone of Lost Cause religion. The purity, innocence, and respectability that southern womanhood evoked for white men were an *essential* part of the social apparatus and logic that kept Black men and women in subjection and fear. As a symbol of the racist South, white southern women provided order through their domestic lives and their bodies. The practices of religiosity, respectability, and homemaking that they cultivated reflected genteel morality and emphasized the sacredness of a particular type of family life and structure. These women, existing virtually on a pedestal, were seen as the virginal ideal of home and hearth. This image was juxtaposed with stereotypes of freed Black women, who were considered sexually promiscuous, impure, and not in need of protection. Black men were understood to be dangerous brutes and rapists, essentially uncontrollable. These racist tropes were used not only to continue to subject the newly freed to danger and ridicule but also to promote violence as a way to maintain order and protect white womanhood.

In this Reconstruction and Redemption southern society, order and purity were maintained through violence. Just after the close of the Civil War, in 1865, the Ku Klux Klan formed in Pulaski, Tennessee. In its earliest days, the purpose of the Klan was to defend white rights, oppose liberty for freed Blacks, and eliminate the Republican Party (at that time the party of emancipation and the Union). The first grand wizard was the former Confederate general Nathan Bedford Forrest. The men (and the women who supported them) in the earliest iteration of the KKK burned crosses and terrorized Republican leaders and voters in the South. They also burned Black churches and schools and made it a point to terrorize northern missionaries who traveled to the South to assist with Reconstruction and education. Ulysses S. Grant pushed the Enforcement Acts through Congress in order to break up this first iteration of the organization.

The KKK returned in 1915 under the aegis of a former Methodist minister, William J. Simmons. Kicking off this second iteration of the organization, Simmons and sixteen other men lit a cross on top of Stone Mountain in Georgia on November 25, 1915, pledging allegiance to the Constitution, American ideals, *and the tenets of the Christian religion.* As Kelly Baker, a scholar of religion and the KKK, has written, "The Klan wanted a homogenous, Protestant white America, free from the corrupting influences of diversity, whether political, religious or social." This reboot of the Klan, steeped in evangelical religion, proved popular not only in the South but across the United States. The new Klan, reinvigorated by racism and anti-immigration sentiment, staged pageants and parades across the country. Notably, the Klan staged a large march in Washington, D.C., on August 8, 1925, that drew 30,000 members to march down Pennsylvania Avenue. At the end of the march, with rain threatening, district dragon L. A. Mueller proclaimed to the assembled Klansmen and audience, "I have faith enough in the Lord that he is with every Klansman. You ought to have as much faith in him as I have. We have never had a drop of rain in Washington when we got down on our knees." Almost immediately, a downpour began. The crowd dispersed quickly.

Historically, it was nothing out of the ordinary for such a violent group as the KKK to center its rhetoric and actions around God and nation. The White League, formed on March 1, 1874, as a paramilitary group of southern Democrats, many of them former Confederate soldiers, adopted similar tactics. The league's platform was clear: "Disregarding all minor questions of principle or policy, and having solely in view the maintenance of our hereditary civilization and Christianity menaced by a stupid Africanization, we appeal to men of our race, of whatever language or nationality, to unite with us against that supreme danger." In other words, the league existed to protect Christianity and civilization against freed Black people and the whites who assisted them. The league spread throughout Louisiana and surrounding states. Its members murdered a seventeen-year-old Black schoolteacher and, later, six white Republicans and twenty Black men in Coushatta, Louisiana. Under the guise of order, league members also hindered any attempt to help newly freed Blacks. Like the KKK, the White League was put down by the Enforcement Acts, but its members simply joined local and state governments, police departments, and militia organizations.

Both the KKK and the White League justified their violent acts through a combination of Christian imagery and calls for a return to the "order" of the slave-owning South. It did not matter that burning churches and murder were crimes. These activities were considered to be in the service of the religious ideal of restoration, of bringing back what white southerners considered the God-given right of white men to rule over all. Although the KKK and the White League were disbanded, white men still formed night-rider groups to terrorize African Americans and anyone else not adhering to the white supremacist norms of the South. Appeals to violence were couched in the language of "civilization" and closely connected to ideas of biblical retribution and God's favor. The ideal of "order," which would evolve into evangelical calls for "law and order," stemmed from harmful stereotypes about African Americans' tendency toward violence and the supposed insubordination of people who merely wanted their freedom and their humanity respected. All of this facilitated the most horrific form of violence done in the name of God and nation from Reconstruction to the civil rights era: lynching.

"The Southern rite of Human Sacrifice" is what historian Don Mathews called it. Lynching was the ultimate method of violence used in the South to punish transgressors—often Black men falsely accused of raping or "insulting" white girls and women—and as a scare tactic to keep African Americans and others from challenging social norms. According to a report by the Equal Justice Initiative in 2017, there were over 4,400 lynchings of Black people in America from 1877 to 1950—a figure that includes 800 more lynchings than had previously been recognized.

Lynching became the ultimate murderous tool used to support white supremacy. Evangelical Christians and churches engaged in lynchings, attending and cheering brutal spectacles of murder enacted upon Black bodies. Many took body parts of the lynched, such as fingers and toes, as souvenirs of the horrendous events, and others sold postcards of mutilated and burned Black men and women. Mathews describes the murder of Sam Hose, an infamous lynching that occurred in 1899, as a form of "sanctified vengeance." Religion, according to Mathews, did not cause lynching. Rather, lynching was *itself* religion.

While it may be difficult to stomach the idea that evangelical Christians participated in these events, it is not difficult to believe if you consider that lynching is a continuation of the horrors of slavery. Violence against Black people continued as an integral and inseparable part of southern life, religion, and culture. Amy Louise Wood's account in her book *Lynching and Spectacle* offers a bracing, shameful retelling of the lynching of Harris Tunstal in Oxford, Mississippi, behind a Methodist Episcopal church. Accused of raping a young white woman in 1885, Tunstal's subsequent lynching is a stark reminder of how white Christian men took part in human judgment and sacrifice with only themselves as jury. A crowd of white men that had gathered in the town square decided, after a hasty outdoor trial of Tunstal by members of the crowd, that since it was Sunday, the town square was not the appropriate place for the lynching. Wood describes their choice to move the lynching to the church as embracing "the holy sensibility of the day, to merge the mob's symbolic act of vengeance with the divine justice enacted in the evangelical church." Tunstal was permitted to pray before the men killed him.

This agonizing history of enslaved and freed African Americans at the hands of evangelical Christians exposes the unsavory foundations of deeply held evangelical beliefs. A literal interpretation of the Bible that deemed slavery as being allowed by God, a mythological ideal of southern civilization based in whiteness, and a preoccupation with purity and sexuality all brought out the worst in white southerners fighting to keep a dishonorable way of life intact. The lives of enslaved and later freed African Americans were made intolerable by evangelicals invested in keeping them in their places and maintaining white supremacy and power.

And while many evangelicals, particularly from the North, genuinely wanted to help the newly freed with education and domestic training, much of the "home missions" work these white believers did was affected by ideas about the superiority of white European civilization and a sense of Christian duty that at times was expressed in ways that demeaned the very people they wished to help. Most of these beliefs were the very same beliefs supporting and enabling violence against Black bodies.

This account is part of the history of evangelicalism. The nineteenth-century racial practices of white supremacy and violence would affect how twentieth-century evangelical leadership engaged African Americans and their forthcoming quest for civil rights, justice, and full citizenship. Most of all, they would allow white evangelical leaders to justify their decision to keep the reins of religious, social, and political power in white men's hands.

2

SAVING THE NATION

Fervor, Fear, and Challenges to Jim Crow

If evangelicals believed in saints, Billy Graham would be balanced at the top. Friend to American presidents and evangelist to the world, Graham became the face of American Christianity over the course of a life that lasted a century. His brand of Christian fervor, fear, and fatalism defined American evangelicalism from the 1940s to the 1970s. He exemplified a kind of religion that combined Christianity, patriotism, and politics into a potent mix of respectability that was predicated on fear of the other. The other, for Graham and his followers, often was communists, Catholics, and immigrants. Graham convincingly instilled in his vast audiences an urgent sense that only by means of their individual salvations through Christ could *America* be saved.

But Graham also preached about race in America. "Only when Christ comes again will little white children of Alabama walk hand in hand with little Black children," he famously said in 1963, when asked to comment on Martin Luther King Jr.'s "I Have a Dream" speech. Women, immigrants, and people of color, especially African Americans, were expected to wait in docile obedience for their turn to achieve the freedoms available to white, male, Anglo-Saxon Protestants. Evangelicals' quest to win the world for Christ—a quest promoted by a white male leadership exemplified by Graham—was to save souls and make believers of all races conform to white, Western Christian ideals. Their quest helped dramatically to solidify for postwar America the racism that was embedded in evangelical beliefs, behaviors, and social prohibitions from the nineteenth and early twentieth centuries.

The creation of twentieth-century evangelicalism —and its relationship to racial politics—are best interpreted through the story of its greatest representative, Billy Graham, "America's White Jesus," as Bob Moser put it in *Rolling Stone*. In life, Graham's staunch sense of morality, his friendships with presidents, and his good looks gained him accolades. Born a Presbyterian, Graham rose to prominence in the 1940s alongside the beginnings of many evangelical organizations as part of a movement known as the "new evangelicalism." Between 1945 and 1970, newly born evangelical groups emerged from institutions such as Fuller Theological Seminary in Pasadena, California. Magazines like *Christianity Today* promoted a forward-thinking Christianity that was not as staid as the fundamentalist versions of earlier times. In a striking shift, these new evangelical believers were willing to engage the world, media, and scholarship.

By looking at the new evangelicalism through the lens of Billy Graham and his contemporaries, we see a clear picture of the lines that evangelicals drew around racial, social, and political issues. They held on to their fundamentalist racial ideologies but, under the guise of "Americanist" culture and obedience to the law, updated them to soften the edges. While evangelicals and fundamentalists battled each other over theology and scripture, their cultural and social racism held them together.

Though their alliance was fragile, evangelicals and fundamentalists shared common ground in their rejection of communism and racial integration and the promotion of male leadership—and Billy Graham was the bridge for the alliance among believers. Graham's rise to prominence and his accomplishments in establishing evangelical political power help to reveal the racial underpinnings of evangelicalism in the twentieth century.

Graham's ascendancy occurred against the backdrop of evangelical organizing in response to modernity. As evangelicals formed themselves into parachurch organizations and engaged in political activity, entering into the print and television world, their grip on the cultural and social visions they wanted to promote was pointedly circumscribed not by racial inclusivity but by racial exclusivity. This exclusivity, which translated to the outside world as a form of belief, was about high boundaries and conformity. American Christians were encouraged by the new evangelicalism to adhere to particular political and social beliefs. With Graham's ascension and the organizing of evangelicals into universities, seminaries, and parachurch groups, the political action they engaged in set them up to claim new power while also placing them, as we shall see, in opposition to the movement for civil and social rights for African Americans.

The National Association of Evangelicals (NAE), founded in 1942, was one of the first major organizations to grow out of the new evangelicalism. It was formed in part because of the difficulty of getting broadcast airtime. Harold Ockenga, a Congregational minister, and J. Elwin Wright, a Pentecostal minister, hoped that a national group of evangelical ministers could bolster claims to the local radio airtime that was being given primarily to representatives of the Federal Council of Churches (FCC), a strong ecumenical organization of mainline Protestants and other progressive Christians.

Smaller evangelical churches and groups outside the FCC were having difficulty obtaining airtime because the FCC blocked its sale to smaller Protestant denominations.

Ockenga and Wright hosted a planning meeting, inviting pastors to Chicago in 1941, and out of that initial meeting the NAE was officially formed in St. Louis the following year. The formation of the NAE was a significant moment in the growth of evangelicalism and its politics in America. The NAE brought under its umbrella evangelical denominations like Lutherans, conservative Presbyterians, Baptists, Methodists, and Congregationalists as well as Pentecostal churches like the Assemblies of God. Including Pentecostals was a milestone, signaling their acceptance into the mainstream after decades of being considered adherents of a backward, backwoods religion. The new organization grew rapidly from fifteen member churches in 1943 to more than thirty-two denominations and over a million members by 1960. The NAE was very white and very male—and would remain so for decades.

At the NAE's founding, no Black denominations were represented, even though major Black denominations such as the National Baptist Convention and the Church of God in Christ could have easily signed the statement of belief. Segregation was not just for housing or buses but for churches as well.

The NAE's infrastructure of church members

and leaders helped to establish a strong foundation for evangelicals, drawing them together and providing a platform for preachers like Billy Graham. The NAE not only represented the evangelical interests of the various denominational members but also became a clearinghouse for evangelical culture and political activity. It was the first of many evangelical organizations to exist outside of traditional churches, promoting both Christ and cultural agendas that fit into the evangelical belief framework.

In the meantime, World War II had a profound effect on American evangelicals. With men going off to war and the rise of Nazi Germany and communism, fears of "the last days" and the coming of the Antichrist gave new urgency to evangelical preachers' messages. Radio shows like Charles Fuller's *Old Fashioned Revival Hour*, broadcast into the homes of Black and white Christians alike, gained popularity and spread the evangelical Christian message. As the war drew to an end, a new threat rose to prominence in the minds of many evangelical Christians: communism. Ministers like Graham were ready to meet that threat.

During the war years, Graham had attended Wheaton College, "the evangelical Harvard." He enrolled there after spending a semester at a fundamentalist Bible school in Florida and taking a few classes at Bob Jones University. He met his wife, Ruth, at Wheaton and after graduation pastored for a time. In 1945, he began working for

Youth for Christ (YFC), Torrey Johnson's newly founded evangelistic organization, and here Graham's ministry took off as he preached at YFC meetings all across the United States. While built on fundamentalist principles, YFC was designed to evangelize youth, catering to young people's tastes with lively music and other activities. YFC suited Graham's style. Often preaching with a newspaper in one hand and a microphone in the other, he became very popular with YFC's constituents.

Graham's success at YFC indeed led to his breakthrough to the mainstream. During a time of intense introspection and a wrestling with his call, in 1949 Graham traveled to Los Angeles to hold a series of revival meetings from September through November. These meetings caught the attention of newspaper mogul William Randolph Hearst, who apocryphally ordered his *Los Angeles Examiner* reporters to "puff Graham." Reporters covered the revival and gave Graham unprecedented exposure. In one newsreel of the revival, now posted on YouTube, one can see the throngs gathered at Graham's tent to hear his message of salvation. His prominence burgeoning, Graham soon began a heavy travel schedule of revivals in America and also abroad. He was the first to preach from the steps of the U.S. Capitol in 1952, during an event that was the impetus for the founding later that year of the National Day of Prayer, which continues today.

Graham's preaching focused on Jesus, but at the

same time he was astutely aware of the changing international order of the world and the perceived threat to America from communism.

Understanding how evangelicals heard his preaching against communism is key to understanding how they later came to view the civil rights movement as a potential communistic arm of destruction in America. For evangelicals, communism was not simply a social movement but an atheist movement that, with almost religious fervor, sought to destroy Christianity.

The linkage of communism to resistance and to civil rights had its roots in the Red Summer of 1919, when Black activists were placed under surveillance by J. Edgar Hoover, then leader of the "radical division" of the U.S. Justice Department. Outside Chicago, the drowning in Lake Michigan of a young Black man who had been pelted with rocks after straying into the white section of a swimming area set off a race riot of horrifying proportions. Red Summer violence was intensely racial in character. It erupted across the country in lynchings, church burnings, and bombings of African American communities in the South. Many African Americans fought back, bolstering Hoover's view that it was Blacks who were the danger.

That summer, Hoover ordered his agents to investigate a supposed connection between African Americans fighting against white racialized violence and Bolshevik radical activities. He also began to compile dossiers on participants. As political scientist Charles Henry wrote in a blog post titled "Remembering the Red Summer of 1919," "it seems the government, despite the pleas of the NAACP, was more concerned about possible black links to organized labor than white violence against black citizens." Hoover's unproven theories lingered into the 1950s as the Red Scare gained momentum. Many Black activists working for civil rights were called communists. Martin Luther King Jr. was called a communist. So when Graham preached about the "communist threat" in the 1950s, he amplified a phrase that resonated forcefully with evangelicals and southern-based Christians, given not only their fear of the Soviets but also their fiery concern about the Black civil rights activists who were, to their way of thinking, promoting communist ideas and socialism.

The linkage of communism with civil rights work—combined with evangelicals' fear of the end times and the Antichrist—instilled fear and determination in evangelists and evangelical listeners alike. A sermon Graham delivered at the Los Angeles revival in 1949, drawing on Psalm 94:3, titled "Why God Allows Communism to Flourish and Why God Allows Christians to Suffer," highlights how he explicitly equated the communist scare with the battle of the last days. "The next world war will occur in five years if Christ tarries," he thundered. "It will make the first two look like a little fight. This world war will sweep civilization into oblivion unless Christ comes and stops it. It's on its way."

The threat of communism fit neatly with the idea of the "end times" that evangelicals believed would bring Jesus Christ back to earth. The threat also was useful in promoting the evangelical idea that individual salvation, rather than collective action such as socialism or civil rights, would stem social and political ills, including communism. Likening the end times to the communist threat, Graham stressed the dual importance of personal salvation and resistance to communism.

In the 1949 Los Angeles revival sermon, he also linked the power of Christianity to love for America and nationalism, arguing that "prayer and spiritual revival" were strong "weapons against communism." "The most effective weapon against communism," he declared, "is to be a born-again Christian . . . because you will never find a true born-again Christian who is a communist or a fellow traveler. You get a man born again, and he will turn from communism." In Graham's understanding, true Christian born-again believers could not possibly hold communist views.

While for white evangelicals personal salvation was the first order of business, during this era the second order was for born-again Americans to embrace "Americanism" as a way to protect the nation and its citizens from the communist threat. Simply put, "Americanism" meant pride in the nation, in the founders, in the Declaration of Independence and the Constitution—and, most important, in the idea that America was a nation ordained by God to save the world. In a 1956 pamphlet titled *Americanism*, Graham outlined his beliefs about America's place in world affairs, noting the founders' insertion of God in all aspects of the founding documents and arguing that the most pressing issues of the day could not be solved unless the nation turned to God: "This nation has the greatest responsibility, obligation and opportunity in the history of the world. However, we are in danger of losing our world-wide prestige unless we can turn to God in such great numbers that our divorce rate will decline, our race problem can be solved, and our crime statistics can be improved." For Graham, then, the idea of Americanism connected directly to the morality of the nation. Graham wanted to bring the nation back to God by invoking God's role in its "divine history." If an American citizen did not live morally and become saved, then the nation as well as the individual would suffer. Graham's take on the linked fate of citizens, government, and nation held the seeds of a nationalistic Christianity, predicated on Christian morals and beliefs as the cornerstone and foundation of the nation, despite the fact that the founders wanted religious freedom for people of all faiths.

Americanism combined patriotism and civic

engagement—and whiteness. Despite all of the evangelical focus on America as a great and moral nation, the United States still legally segregated African Americans in schools, housing, and innumerable other contexts. Jim Crow was the law of the land. Graham's revival meetings in the South became a site of tension regarding how the race question should be dealt with.

Graham's first integrated meeting took place in 1953 in Chattanooga, Tennessee, but he also held segregated meetings in the South that same year. While Graham told NAE members in 1952 that the church "was on the tail end—to our shame—of progress along racial lines in America today" and that the church "should be leading rather than following," as Steven P. Miller wrote in *Billy Graham and the Rise of the Republican South*, Graham firmly adopted a gradualist approach to race relations. He bemoaned racism as a sin yet offered only small, cosmetic adjustments to change the ethos. Miller notes that Graham's "racial reasoning" featured a color-blind Christology, a defense of the South, an embrace of the southern relational culture, and the denunciation of extremists. I would wrap up Graham's reasoning into what I see as his development of an "evangelical gentility": he recognized the problem of racial injustice and evoked the pain caused by unjust social norms, but he was unwilling to break ranks with the white status quo.

In 1954 an event occurred that would profoundly

affect evangelicals' views on race: the Supreme Court's decision in *Brown v. Board of Education*. This landmark decision mandating school desegregation launched one of the defining civil rights battles of the era. In response, many evangelicals took their children out of public school rather than have them attend with African Americans. Churches and other evangelical organizations founded "segregation academies," private religious schools that were tax-exempt. In Virginia and other states, local policies of "massive resistance" to *Brown* encouraged schools to consider desegregating while, at the same time, turning to state courts to deter the *Brown* mandate. These moves were the beginning of long, protracted battles, first against desegregation and later against busing. They did not, however, slow down the momentum of the civil rights movement.

The Montgomery bus boycott that began in December 1955 put Martin Luther King Jr. in a position of prominence on the national and international stage. The boycott created a stark juxtaposition between Graham's moderate stance on the issue of integration and King's principled, nonviolent activism. Rosa Parks's defiant stance in refusing to give up her seat on a bus was just the first in a series of events that led to the boycott in Montgomery, spearheaded by the Montgomery Improvement Association. King, who had completed his doctorate at Boston University, was invited to come to

45

Montgomery to support the boycott, and from December 1955 to December 1956, he did, promoting a strategy of nonviolent action. Despite attempts by local businessmen to break up the boycott and the bombing of King's home in Montgomery, the boycott resulted in the desegregation of buses through the *Browder v. Gayle* decision, upheld by the Supreme Court in 1956.

During the boycott, President Dwight D. Eisenhower asked Billy Graham to reach out to both Black and white ministers about the racial issue. Graham did so but did little else to assist. The successful end of the boycott resulted in King becoming a national figure, and only then did Graham invite him to give the invocation at the famous Madison Square revival on July 18, 1957. Later that year, Graham invited Howard Jones to join his Billy Graham Evangelistic Association team as its first Black minister. According to undocumented reports, Jones told Graham, "Everything in your meetings is white— the choir, the speakers, the audience—everything!" While the Madison Square revival was lauded in the press, King asked Graham the following year to refrain from appearing on stage with noted segregationist and Texas governor Price Daniel. Graham refused King's request. It was the beginning of a testy relationship between Graham and King. It also clearly marked Graham's characteristic waffling about the civil rights movement.

Graham worried about the increasing levels of

civil disobedience deployed in the civil rights movement. He had hoped to see the movement continue to advocate for change via the justice system, not through civil disobedience, even if it was nonviolent. Eventually, Graham began to take tougher stances against King's efforts. He was especially disdainful after the March on Washington in August 1963, when he made the aforementioned remarks about King's "Dream" speech—that it would take the second coming of Christ before we would see white children walk hand in hand with Black children.

This disdain for King and the civil rights movement connected Graham to other prominent evangelicals of the 1950s and 1960s. Billy James Hargis, a fundamentalist who embraced segregation and anticommunism, was especially hard on King and communism, invariably linking the two together. In his book series *One Minute before Midnight! (A Christian Americanism Book in Three Parts)*, Hargis predicted the imminent fall of America to communism if souls were not saved and communism not defeated. "Today, America is at war with Communism," he wrote. "This is a struggle to the end, between Decency and evil. Communism Hates God. Communism Seeks the destruction of the Church and the Bible. For that Reason, Russia Hates the United States. This beloved Christian Nation is God's last Stronghold for Christianity." Laden with apocalyptic imagery and fears of God subjecting

47

the nation to communism if morality were not restored, Hargis's book resonated with evangelicals. For Hargis, a vast range of organizations appeared red-tinted or pink-hued, including Yale Divinity School, the National Council of Churches, and other churches that he deemed "socialist." Hargis preached to his listeners, "Every time your church loses another freedom—we are coming closer and closer to the commie vision of a Protestant Catholic church with red leadership."

Hargis was completely transparent about arguing that communism held another threat to conservative Christians of the 1950s: it would upset the "social order," a reference to racial desegregation. Describing Martin Luther King Jr. as a "Stinking Racial Adjuratory and a communist," Hargis believed, like Carl McIntire and others who promoted Americanism, that desegregation violated biblical principles. In her book *What's Fair on the Air?*, Heather Hendershot demonstrates that in the fifties and sixties opposition to desegregation played a role in virtually every political issue that lured fundamentalists like Hargis into politics.

With the founding of the John Birch Society by Robert Welch in 1958, conservatives who were religious and opposed communism and civil rights found a new home. The society was named after American missionary John Birch, who had been killed by Mao Zedong's People's Liberation Army in 1945. Staunchly opposed to the United Nations and to U.S.-Soviet cooperation, and a hard charger for Americanism, the John Birch Society also took a hard line against integration. Both Carl McIntire and Billy James Hargis became Birchers, and the group benefited from broad appeal across denominations and faiths, early on even drawing in some Mormon members. A group called the White Citizens' Council put up over 200 billboards in the South showing a photo of King at Tennessee's Highlander Center accompanied by the erroneous headline "Martin Luther King at a Communist Training School." Hargis later used this line in his pamphlet *Unmasking Martin Luther King, Jr. the Deceiver*.

Other southern evangelicals were just as vocal in preaching about segregation, including Southern Baptist W. A. Criswell, pastor of First Baptist Church in Dallas, Texas. Criswell was Billy Graham's pastor after Graham joined this church in 1953 following his revivals in Dallas. An unyielding segregationist, Criswell declared in a message delivered to the South Carolina Baptist Evangelism conference in February 1956, that "true Ministers must passionately resist government mandated desegregation because it is a denial of ALL that we believe in." In what was called the "fiery sermon," this statement of Criswell's stance was welcomed by some in the Southern Baptist denomination, though others remained wary. Writing about Criswell in the *Journal of Southern Religion*, Curtis

Freeman notes that Criswell's speech so impressed then governor George Bell Timmerman Jr. that he invited Criswell to address the South Carolina state legislature the next day. Senator Strom Thurmond introduced Criswell to his fellow lawmakers, and as a result the lawmakers passed a resolution asking the U.S. attorney general to put the NAACP on the Justice Department's watch list and to ban NAACP members from government employment. For his part, Graham told reporters after the South Carolina speech, "Criswell and I have never seen eye to eye on the race question." Yet it was Criswell who would express a change of heart in June 1968 upon being elected president of the Southern Baptist Convention, inviting Blacks through an "open door" to attend First Baptist Church of Dallas. Freeman rightly notes that the manner in which Criswell narrated this change of heart was a "generalized confession, lacking any content as to racial guilt," and offering "only regret and not repentance"—far from a complete conversion to supporting racial equality and civil rights.

Evangelicals were concerned not only about integration but also about interference from other religious groups, notably Catholics. This became abundantly clear in the 1960 presidential election, in which Catholic John F. Kennedy ran against Vice President Richard Nixon. Graham was at the forefront of the Kennedy opposition, even holding a secret meeting of prominent pastors in Montreux,

Switzerland, in August 1960 to plan how to mobilize against the candidate. These same pastors met a few days later in New York City without Graham, having selected Norman Vincent Peale, author of *The Power of Positive Thinking* and pastor of the Marble Collegiate Church (which Donald Trump later attended), to be the face of their coalition. Peale, a notorious anti-Catholic, told the gathered ministers, "Our American culture is at stake. I don't say it won't survive, but it won't be what it was."

According to his biographer, Carol George, Peale met with the press after this gathering and shared a group statement indicting the character of the Roman Catholic Church. The event backfired, however, giving Kennedy the opening he needed to deliver a speech to the Greater Houston Ministerial Association on September 12, 1960, in which he assured the gathered Protestant ministers and others that his Catholic faith would not get in the way of his decision-making as president of the United States: "I believe in an America that is officially neither Catholic, Protestant, nor Jewish; where no public official either requests or accepts instructions on public policy from the Pope, the National Council of Churches, or any other ecclesiastical source."

Kennedy's subsequent win did not eliminate anti-Catholic bias or heal political divisions, but the mobilization of evangelicals against Kennedy's candidacy clearly put religion-based power brokering into the presidential mainstream: Kennedy made sure to be seen with Billy Graham at a golf game right before his inauguration in 1961.

Evangelical preoccupation with race, communism, and Catholicism would only ramp up in the 1960s. On the one hand, evangelicals wanted souls to be saved. On the other, they wanted everyone to stay in their places. Graham gained prominence in American society in part through his ability to peer into the minds of his followers and to perceive how they wished to see the world. So it was no surprise when Graham did not attend the March on Washington in 1963. In an Associated Press wire dated August 28, Graham warned that some "extremists are going too fast" with regard to integration. In the same remarks, he also noted that "racial prejudice is a two-way street. It must be ended and Christian love must prevail." How that would ever come about remained unanswered. Graham's suggestion that Christ, rather than the government, was responsible for altering the social strata and making racism obsolete encapsulates beautifully how evangelicals of the time thought about race. In this time, in this era—on this issue—it was not the purpose of evangelicals to work for social change, because it was God who would eventually make that change—no matter that "God," for many Americans, was envisioned as the white, blond Jesus depicted by Warner Sallman.

Evangelicals were frightened, moreover, that

God was beginning to be erased from public schools. With the *Engel v. Vitale* decision in 1962, ruling that school-led prayer violated the First Amendment, and the *Abington v. Schempp* decision in 1963, ruling unconstitutional the requirement that students read the Bible and say the Lord's Prayer in public school settings, evangelical fears of communism intensified. Graham expressed these fears at a crusade in 1963, declaring that secularism "is the fastest-growing religion in America." He warned that if the Supreme Court continued its trend toward throwing God and the Bible out of "our national life," a huge march on Washington dwarfing the civil rights march might result.

The issues of religion and secularism in the public sphere, rising violence and civil disobedience in the civil rights movement, and the escalation of the war in Vietnam all combined to inspire ministers to speak out against the increasingly common protest practices of organizing and marching. Jerry Falwell gave his "Ministers and Marches" speech, in which he condemned Martin Luther King Jr. and other ministers engaged in protesting and marching for civil rights, on March 21, 1965, the same day on which King and other Black and white ministers were walking across the Edmund Pettus Bridge in Selma, Alabama. Falwell criticized the civil rights movement, declaring that "preachers are not called to be politicians but soul winners." He would later apologize for the sermon, but he seemed to have learned from the very tactics he had criticized, going on to use them quite effectively on behalf of the Moral Majority, which he founded in the late 1970s.

During these years, whether put into play by major evangelical figures like Graham or by local organizations like White Citizens' Councils or the NAE, the strategies with which evangelicals dealt with racism were conflicted. Racism could be acknowledged as a sin but one in which only Christ himself would intervene. Gradualism, not marches or legislation mandating integration, was the proper Christian way to effect change. This was a gradualism that would have to be mediated by what evangelicals and fundamentalists believed was God's will. At the same time, evangelicals also believed that their religious values, their "new evangelicalism," should be drawn into governing in a kind of Christian nationalism—or, as it was called at the time, "Americanism." This would provide a way to fight back against godless communism and the forces of change seeking to destroy their America.

At the center of this battle stood Billy Graham. He was the exemplar of the "new evangelicalism," helping to establish the outlines of what would develop into a tight and ongoing relationship among evangelicals, politics, and the presidency.

As the 1960s drew to a close, evangelical anxiety heated up. The passage of civil rights legislation, the assassinations of Martin Luther King Jr. and Robert Kennedy, and the riots at the Democratic National Convention in 1968 all helped to precipitate a shift, whereby evangelical ideas and beliefs about race would begin to harden and take on new contours. It would take more than simply ignoring race for evangelicals to continue to hold political power and sway. It would take a whole new approach to hold power, while putting a coat of fresh paint on the old racist structures of evangelical life and belief.

3

WHITEWASHING RACISM
AND THE RISE OF THE
RELIGIOUS RIGHT

"Preachers are not called to be politicians but soul winners," Jerry Falwell declared in his "Ministers and Marches" speech delivered in March of 1965. In condemning Christian involvement in politics, Falwell was criticizing Martin Luther King Jr.'s advocacy of the civil rights movement. Would Falwell have been surprised, if he could have looked into a crystal ball, that by 1979 he himself would be leading a movement called the Moral Majority, a movement explicitly teamed up with Republican Party politics and political action?

In fact, what Falwell condemned in 1965 would become the bedrock of evangelical organizing in the 1970s and beyond. While abortion is commonly understood as the issue that began to unite evangelicals in the 1970s, I give that dubious honor to the issue of race. Race hatred played the fundamental role in, first, pushing evangelicals toward a "color-blind" gospel, which would provide cover for their racially motivated organizing against the federal government, and, second, their push to block implementation of the hard-won gains of the civil rights movement. This color-blind gospel is how evangelicals used biblical scripture to affirm that everyone, no matter what race, is equal and that race does not matter. The reality of the term "color-blind," however, was more about making Black and other ethnic evangelicals conform to whiteness and accept white leadership as the norm both religiously and socially. It is the equivalent of today's oft-quoted phrase "I don't see color." Saying that means white is the default color.

For evangelicals, the years from the seventies to the nineties were defining ones, encompassing their cultural acquiescence to the inclusion of African Americans in their churches, revivals, and schools while simultaneously fighting against the gains of the civil rights movement in the political and legal arena. Holding on to racist ideologies, including prohibitions against race mixing, dating, and marriage, evangelicals embraced an intransigence that spurred them on to political activism and organizing—the very thing for which Falwell had come down on King just a few years earlier. Using morality and color-blind conservatism as a shield, evangelicals made new political alliances and created organizations, such as the Moral Majority, that would promote their favored issues while continuing to embrace racist practices and strategies to consolidate economic and political power.

Race loomed large and posed significant challenges for evangelicals as the 1970s unrolled. The civil rights movement had produced two major pieces of legislation, the Civil Rights Act of 1964 and the Voting Rights Act of 1965, both of which worked alongside other substantial governmental and cultural changes to dismantle the Jim Crow–era restrictions under which vast numbers of African Americans lived. Churches of various evangelical denominations, including Southern Baptist, were forced to rethink their stances on segregation. The result was their conception of and eager adoption of "color-blind conservatism."

Color-blind conservatism rested on the idea that since the government was "taking care" of race reform, there was no need for conservatives to discuss racial issues in depth, detail, or sincerity. Historian Darren Dochuk showed in *From Bible Belt to Sunbelt* how Southern Baptists and Billy Graham skillfully applied this strategy—Dochuk calls it a "color-blind gospel"—as early as the aftermath of the 1965 Watts riots. In the three years after the riots and before the racial unrest of the summer of 1968, Southern Baptists reached out to the National Baptist Convention in a replay of the late nineteenth century to hold "Race Relations Sundays," when white and Black Baptist churches would "share" their pulpits and sermons. These efforts served as a precursor to the gradual integration of religious services and programming over the 1970s.

The general expectation of white evangelicals in both the nineteenth and the twentieth centuries was that nonwhite believers would *take on* the practices and viewpoints of white members and leadership, no matter the cultural contexts in which Black evangelicals had been born or raised. As a result, tensions surrounding race and ethnicity commonly lodged in harsh criticism of Black cultural practices of dress, singing, or worship expressions. In order for Black evangelicals to belong, they had to emulate whiteness.

William Bentley, the second president of the National Negro Evangelical Association, which was founded in 1963, suggested that this was rarely a problem, because Black evangelicals, and particularly the Black evangelical leadership of the 1960s, were "part and parcel of the institutions in which they received their training." In other words, for Bentley and the Black fundamentalists, Black Pentecostals, and Black graduates of evangelical schools his organization represented, Black evangelicals could not "be expected to articulate a black ethnic viewpoint," given the dominance of conservative, white-led institutions in this religious world.

But in no way did all Black evangelicals agree with Bentley. At least two major Black evangelicals of the 1960s directly engaged white believers on their racism.

The first was Tom Skinner. Raised in a middle-class Black family, Skinner had been a good student by day and, unbeknownst to his parents, a gang leader in Harlem by night before he had a profound conversion experience, which he recounted in his 1968 book *Black and Free*. In 1970, after Skinner had become popular on the evangelical circuit, he was asked to speak at the Urbana 70 Student Missions Conference meeting sponsored by Inter-Varsity Christian Fellowship, an evangelical college organization. His speech, "The U.S. Racial Crisis and World Evangelism," powerfully and prophetically confronted the racism and "Americanism," or perhaps more to the point, white nationalism, of evangelicals. Here are Skinner's words:

Understand that for those of us in the Black community, it was not the evangelical who came and taught us our worth and dignity as Black men. It was not the Bible-believing fundamentalist who stood up and told us that Black was beautiful. It was not the evangelical who preached to us that we should stand on our own two feet and be men, be proud that Black was beautiful, and that God could work his life out through our redeemed Blackness. Rather, it took Stokely Carmichael, Rap Brown, and the Brothers to declare to us our dignity. God will not be without a witness.

Skinner's speech caused a considerable buzz in evangelical circles. *Christianity Today*, in its January 29, 1971, issue, reported that more than 400 Black evangelical students had attended the meeting and noted that "Skinner has not shrunk from denouncing aspects of white middle-class evangelicalism that seemed to him contrary to scripture."

One of Skinner's friends was Bill Pannell, who came out of the Black Plymouth Brethren tradition. Pannell joined Skinner's crusades in 1968 and became part of his ministry. Already a traveling evangelist and speaker, Pannell published a book titled *My Friend, the Enemy* in 1968 chronicling his experiences as a Black man in America around both racism and Christianity. Commenting on the efforts of white evangelicals to practice color-blind conservatism, Pannell wrote: "I have no trouble believing you want me in your church to sing on Sunday. I have very little faith that you want me in your living room for serious discussion. Yet here is where the breakthrough may take place." Pannell, a product of what he called "mulatto" parents, also pointedly addressed intermarriage, a core issue for evangelicals. In a chapter called "Now about Your Daughter," Pannell wrote poignantly of evangelicals' fear of sex and "negro" men: "The ghost of negro sex prowess and white female purity still mocks us in the closets of our minds. Neither Protestant theology nor education has dispelled it. Bible Belt Fundamentalism, which served as midwife when it was born, serves even now to nurse it in its old age."

Pannell's book offered an honest, blunt reflection, by an evangelical in the tradition, on the broader social and cultural prohibitions from the nineteenth century that persisted despite evangelicals' slow moves to improve race relations. The changes occurring in the late 1960s were cosmetic rather than deep. One reason for their limited scope was evangelicals' strong opposition to interracial marriage and support for miscegenation laws, which had only recently been struck down by the Supreme Court decision in *Loving v. Virginia* in 1967. The hot-button issue of interracial relationships would prove to be an important factor in how evangelicals would eventually come together to develop an unprecedented kind of political activism and, at the same time, to form a formidable voting bloc. Ground zero for that battle would be located at a bulwark of nationalism and biblical fundamentalism—Bob Jones University.

Bob Jones Sr. was a fundamentalist preacher

who in 1927 founded a university in his own name to offer a biblical education, to promote "Western civilization," and, very important, to avoid all mention of evolution. Originally located in Florida, Bob Jones University moved to Cleveland, Tennessee, during the Depression, and enrollment grew steadily. After World War II, the student population increased dramatically, and the university made a final move to Greenville, South Carolina, where the founder's son, Bob Jones Jr., took on increasing responsibility.

As staunch defenders of Americanism, father and son began to run national conferences that had the word "Americanism" in their names. These were staged for the benefit of both the students and the general public. At a 1952 conference, Bob Jones Sr. remarked: "I am not so disturbed about the enemy bombs that may be dropped on us as I am about the termites of moral decay in the foundation of our American Society. The germ of communism can never destroy the body of our democracy except as that body is already sick with degeneracy and immorality. I believe in arming America, but it is more important that America be strong in the Lord and in the power of his might."

By the 1970s, the main concerns of the Jones patriarchs shifted, as the founder's grandson Bob Jones III worried less about immorality and its relationship to communism than he did about interracial relationships. The prohibition against interracial relationships drew on both cultural and biblical traditions. Many evangelicals and fundamentalists still clung to nineteenth-century beliefs regarding scripture, including admonitions in the Hebrew Bible to Israelites not to mix with "other" people. In a concession to the times, the university began to accept students of Asian heritage, but only those who signed the university's statement of faith promising not to participate in interracial dating. The university board opposed enrolling Black men and women due to concerns about interracial dating and marriage. With the passage of the Civil Rights Act and other legislation of the 1960s, however, it became problematic for the university to hold on to these prohibitions. Here, in Bob Jones University's reluctance to give up its rules about race mixing, the school became an unwitting catalyst for evangelical political activism.

In a *Politico* article called "The Real Origins of the Religious Right," historian Randall Balmer debunked one of the most durable myths in recent history, the conceit that the religious right, fundamentalism, and conservative evangelicals emerged as a political movement in response to the Supreme Court decision in *Roe v. Wade* in 1973. Racism, not abortion, explains why evangelicals came together to pursue political action, a process that came about with a push from Paul Weyrich, one of the founders in 1973 of the Heritage Foundation, along with Edwin Feulner, Joseph Coors, and other political operatives. In fact, it was the stripping of tax-exempt status from Bob Jones University following its loss of a civil rights case brought by African American parents in Holmes County, Mississippi, in May 1969 that was the catalyst for full-throated evangelical engagement in the political realm.

The case, *Green v. Kennedy*, challenged the applications of three segregated academies for tax-exempt status. When the Supreme Court ruled on the case in 1971, it upheld a new Internal Revenue Service (IRS) policy that forbade racially discriminatory private schools to apply for or receive the federal tax exemption available to charitable and educational institutions. Additionally, the court ruled that donations to these discriminatory institutions would no longer be tax deductible. Bob Jones University was one of the institutions the IRS focused on. When the IRS sent a letter to the university in 1970 asking if it discriminated on the basis of race, the university replied that it did not admit African Americans. The following year, under pressure from the IRS, the university admitted a married African American man. Dr. Bob Jones III spoke of this admission in a conversation with a reporter from the *Greenville News* in 1971, remarking, "Orientals have been accepted to Bob Jones for quite some time, and . . . they [have] accepted the university stipulation that they could not date across racial lines. The reason that blacks had not been admitted before . . . was that the board believed unmarried blacks would refuse to accept the rule (against interracial dating), or agitate to change it if they were admitted." The article also quoted Jones as saying, "We sought a way to help them"—meaning nonwhite students—"without destroying what was already here." That first Black student enrolled at Bob Jones quit after a month, and although the university continued to admit married Black students, it lost its tax-exempt status in 1976 for barring those who were not married.

The story of Bob Jones University does not end there, but let's pause to unpack this story, as it reveals several things about evangelical racism. First, both fundamentalists and evangelicals were terrified of race mixing, a fear that dated back to the Reconstruction and Redemption periods after the Civil War. White women, as we have seen, were put on a pedestal to promote moral and social "purity." Black men were vilified and often lynched over myths about their sexual prowess and their desire for white women. Black women were sexualized and sexually abused by white men who deemed them "loose" or wanton. These tropes from the nineteenth century, coupled with miscegenation laws and readings of scripture, combined to make integration one of the most feared governmental edicts for evangelicals, fundamentalists, and white conservatives. As Bill Pannell pointed out in his book's "Now about Your Daughter" chapter, this fear remained alive and well in the 1970s, though evangelicals rarely spoke of it publicly. Bob Jones University and its leadership simply said the quiet part out loud to the IRS, as Joseph Crespino noted in a chapter titled "Civil Rights and the Religious Right" in *Rightward Bound: Making America Conservative in the 1970s.*

When a number of racially discriminatory schools continued to receive tax exemption, the plaintiffs in *Green v. Kennedy* reopened their case with the IRS. The commissioner of the IRS agreed that the agency's enforcement policies were inadequate. The IRS issued new guidelines with the upshot that schools would need to enroll a significant number of minority students in order to qualify as tax-exempt, with "significant" defined as 20 percent of the minority school-age population in the community the school served.

The court's decision angered evangelicals, and it was Paul Weyrich, the Catholic who founded the Heritage Foundation, who showed them how to harness their anger into political activism. Weyrich's obituary in the *New York Times* in 2008 described him as one of the four pillars of conservatism, alongside William F. Buckley, Barry Goldwater, and Ronald Reagan. That description of him, by conservative direct-mail giant and evangelical Richard A. Viguerie, was well earned. In many ways, Weyrich was the man behind the curtain of modern religious conservative politics.

Weyrich was involved in several conservative movements, but his political philosophy found its apex in his aim to unite Catholics with evangelicals and other conservatives into a powerful voting bloc in order to change society—or, rather, to turn it back to the good old days.

Weyrich supported the notion of the traditional nuclear family, and he believed that government should work on behalf of the family. In 1966 he was press secretary to Republican senator Gordon Allott of Colorado. In the midseventies, through his work with the Heritage Foundation and with financial backing from beer brewer Joseph Coors, Weyrich had established himself as a major conservative player. Though no longer employed as a congressional staffer, he was committed to conservative politics, and he actively looked for a cause that might unite evangelicals into a voting bloc. The IRS decision forbidding tax-exempt status for private schools engaging in racial discrimination provided one.

Evangelicals had already been motivated enough to inundate the IRS with more than 120,000 letters protesting the new policy—enough that the IRS backed off its percentage requirement for proving the integration of Christian schools. This tactic of flooding government offices with letters, phone calls, and, later, emails would become an important part of evangelical political strategy in the 1970s and beyond. As Daniel K. Williams points out in his book *God's Own Party: The Making of the Christian Right*, even Falwell took time away from his anti-gay-rights campaign in 1977 to speak out against the 1971 IRS directive. As Falwell increasingly emphasized morality-focused issues, including pornography, homosexuality, and abortion, on his TV show, *The Old-Time Gospel Hour*, he evolved into an important force fighting against the IRS. Over the next few years, evangelicals mobilized and formed new organizations, including the National Christian Action Coalition and the high-profile Moral Majority. The success of these groups would open the door for a new cottage industry of evangelical organizations taking up morally based political causes for which they would openly lobby in Washington. They would intensively and broadly appeal to evangelicals for support in the form of monthly donations. Much like the televangelists, these now nakedly political groups would become both wealthy and powerful in the process.

The name "Moral Majority" came from Weyrich, who had previously written about how a "moral majority" could "re-create this great nation." In May 1979, Weyrich used the term at a meeting with W. A. Criswell and other evangelical leaders in Dallas. Falwell heard the term and said, "That's it. We're going to be called the Moral Majority." Falwell hosted the organization's headquarters in Lynchburg, Virginia, already home to both Thomas Road Baptist Church and Liberty University. The

Moral Majority started up a monthly newsletter, the *Moral Majority Report*, and used it to promote moral *and* political issues important to evangelicals. Moral had become political.

The Moral Majority then took on an important role in the campaign to elect Ronald Reagan to the presidency in 1980. Evangelicals were not enthusiastic about the incumbent Jimmy Carter, even though he was a born-again Southern Baptist. Many blamed him for the race-tolerant IRS rulings and other policies. Carter was just not one of them, despite his Baptist identity. Carter's interview with *Playboy* in 1976, in which he said honestly that "I've looked on a lot of women with lust. I've committed adultery in my heart many times," was a bridge too far for many evangelicals. Reagan, a former two-term governor of California, on the other hand, attended Donn Moomaw's church, Bel Air Presbyterian—but he also had active connections to many California evangelical networks. He also didn't discuss his first divorce or sex life. Thus Reagan, not Carter, became the evangelical darling.

Weyrich, Falwell, and others did their best to amplify evangelical support for Reagan in the 1980 election, and they invited the candidate to speak to a group of evangelicals in Dallas in August 1980. Reagan shared the Dallas stage with politically interested "new right" evangelicals, including Phyllis Schlafly, Pat Robertson, and Tim LaHaye. Local pastors in attendance included W. A. Criswell and

James Robison, a fiery preacher who railed against homosexuality and communism in his speech. Earlier, Robison had accompanied John Connally to pick up Reagan from the airport, and on the way to the venue Robison told Reagan how to connect with the crowd by giving him this important, and now historic, line: "You can't endorse me, but I endorse you." Reagan's speech, and especially his endorsement of evangelicals, was rapturously received. He closed it by mobilizing the crowd with the line "Vote to protect the American family and respect its interests in the formulation of public policy." Evangelicals were well politicized by this point, and almost all of the ones in Reagan's camp were white.

The most telling moment of that meeting, however, appears in an archived clip of Paul Weyrich's speech at the rally in which he discusses how to mobilize Christian voters by grouping them into "social precincts." In an interview with Bill Moyers, Weyrich defined the idea of the social precinct as the grouping together of voters who believe in the same moral issues, even if they live across town from each other; conservative, religious middle- and upper-class voters, he pointed out, might not have anything in common with the gay person who lives next door to them. (Here, we see shades of the gerrymandering to come.) Weyrich also told the audience that most Christians had "goo goo" syndrome; that is, "good government syndrome—they want everyone to vote." Weyrich backed the *opposite* position: "I don't want everybody to vote. Elections are not won by a majority of people. They never have been from the beginning of our country, and they are not now. As a matter of fact, our leverage in the elections quite candidly goes up as the voting populace goes down." This was in 1980.

Both Reagan and Weyrich did important work at the conference to steer evangelicals toward the Republican Party, introducing what would become important ideas in voter suppression and tacitly expressing underlying racism. Reagan's enthusiastic embrace of evangelicals at the August meeting was just one in a series of signals that he made to all those who believed government had grown too large—especially government that made antiracist decisions. Right before the Weyrich-hosted conference, Reagan made his famous Neshoba County Fair speech, in which he said, "I believe in states' rights." Neshoba County is in Mississippi, and it is the same county in which civil rights workers Michael Schwerner, James Chaney, and Andrew Goodman were murdered during the civil rights movement. Evangelicals and southerners alike understood "states' rights" to mean that individual states, not the federal government, had the right to establish laws, especially laws concerning race.

"States' rights" was a dog whistle for the GOP's "Southern strategy." The Southern strategy was most surgically defined and wielded by Lee Atwater, a notorious political operative best known for his work on the 1988 Bush campaign and the infamous Willie Horton ad, one of history's most racist political ads ever. Before that, he worked on the 1980 Reagan campaign and went to the White House with Reagan as political coordinator. Later, he served as chairman of the Republican National Committee.

In an interview with Alexander Lamis in 1981, which was subsequently reprinted in the *Nation* on November 13, 2012, Atwater outlined his thoughts about what the Southern strategy was in regard to voting—let's call it his political philosophy: "You start out in 1954 by saying, 'Nigger, nigger, nigger.' By 1968 you can't say 'nigger'—that hurts you, backfires. So you say stuff like, uh, forced busing, states' rights, and all that stuff, and you're getting so abstract. Now, you're talking about cutting taxes, and all these things you're talking about are totally economic things and a byproduct of them is, blacks get hurt worse than whites.... 'We want to cut this,' is much more abstract than even the busing thing, uh, and a hell of a lot more abstract than 'Nigger, nigger.'"

Atwater's description of the Southern strategy coupled well with evangelical concerns of morality, economics, and social order. It also went along well with the "color-blind" evangelicalism that had started in the late 1960s. The combination of Atwater's Southern strategy with Weyrich's concept of the social precinct, which was a way to put to-gether like-minded conservatives across a geo-graphic space, would create an important voting juggernaut benefiting conservatives. It mobilized white Christians and at the same time demonized those who would not vote based on their morality or the Republican party line—that is, Democrats. The Southern strategy of using coded words such as "states' rights" and "forced busing," then, would appeal to evangelicals and would be used by them from the 1980s forward.

This epic 1980 Dallas meeting has been described by Sidney Milkis and Daniel Tichenor in their book *Rivalry and Reform* as no less than a marriage be-tween Southern Baptists and Republicans. And I think it is fair to say that it wasn't only Southern Baptists in Dallas who got married to Republicans. Most white evangelicals got married to Republi-cans. This was a marriage that would spawn a lot of children in the form of the groups evangelicals cre-ated to lobby for and promote moral issues. While some have deemed the Moral Majority a failure in terms of influencing Ronald Reagan's presidential politics, it was a success at both galvanizing evan-gelicals and creating offshoot organizations to pro-mote "family issues" that were also invested in in-fluencing education, voting, candidates, and more. In 1977, two major organizations that would prove powerful in the evangelical lobby were formed. That year, Donald Wildmon created the American

Family Association, and James Dobson launched Focus on the Family. Dobson's other organization, the Family Research Council, would be founded in 1981 and incorporated in 1983.

All of these seemingly benign organizations had the specific purpose of lobbying government on evangelical concerns about the family, marriage, abortion, and education. They were also important in fostering an evangelical culture that promoted color-blindness and conservatism. The groups were not overtly racist, and all would at times feature African Americans in promotional materials, on radio shows, and as speakers at conferences. Yet the underlying message of these groups was that morality was essential to preserving the nation and that the sexual immorality of America, including race mixing, would be its downfall. Much like the nineteenth-century admonitions to protect white womanhood and discourage miscegenation, the message from evangelicals, specifically white evangelicals, was that they were poised to save the nation and civilization. If people would follow their lead—including adopting their agendas on abortion, education, voting, and nationalism—America would be much better off than it would be in the egalitarian, openly integrationist future being pursued through the civil rights and youth movements of the sixties and seventies.

The same logic explains why opposition to the Equal Rights Amendment (ERA) became important to evangelicals from the 1970s onward. Maintaining the status quo of white male leadership and traditional family values was important to people like Phyllis Schlafly, a powerfully connected Catholic who held sway with evangelicals. Schlafly was a staunch anticommunist and supporter of the John Birch Society. The themes in her book *A Choice Not an Echo* resonated with many conservative evangelical women in the 1960s. Schlafly viewed the ERA as fundamentally detrimental to the family, and after founding the Eagle Forum in 1972, she used it as the platform for the Stop ERA movement. Schlafly was an important cog in the gears of evangelical political organizing. Due in part to her organization's efforts, the ERA fell short of the number of states needed to ratify it: Schlafly celebrated this on June 30, 1982, with an "Over the Rainbow Dinner."

While all of this activity pushed evangelicals into the political realm, they continued to seek acceptance in the social realm by practicing the colorblind gospel, even as they supported racial separation and white nationalism more or less under the national radar. Oral Roberts, a well-known healing and prosperity evangelist from Oklahoma, provides one example of how this hat trick was done. Roberts was one of many Pentecostals to hold interracial services. When asked about his racially mixed meetings in the 1950s, he replied, "We didn't talk about it, we just did it." Yet at the very same time he often acquiesced to the Jim Crow norms of the cities in which he pitched his tent—much as Billy Graham did.

The 1960s brought about significant changes in Roberts's ministry. He founded Oral Roberts University in 1963 and then later became a United Methodist minister. When the university was formally dedicated in 1967, Billy Graham spoke at the event—he and Roberts had become friends by this time. But Roberts was interested in more than education, and he made his mark as a shrewd purveyor of entertainment and televangelism.

His most interesting foray into the modeling of interracial cooperation, according to Daniel Isgrigg, who served as director of the Holy Spirit Research Center at Oral Roberts University, was a TV variety show called *Contact*. Airing occasionally in prime time beginning in 1969, the show's very first guest was the gospel singer Mahalia Jackson. On that inaugural show, Roberts and Jackson joined hands to pray for God to heal the nation. Isgrigg interpreted this hand-holding as Roberts showing the public that "Jesus was the answer to the problem of race." That might have been part of Roberts's message— but the gesture was also a strikingly clever move on Roberts's part. By holding the hand of this revered Black gospel singer, he attempted to win for himself a broader viewing audience without breaking hard and fast racial norms. Jackson, with her phenomenal singing voice, was not a threat to white

about "Blackness" being a marker of piety, especially to southern church people, and served as an
effective shield against charges of racism in a time
of significant change in race relations. By casting
Black people as "godly" and more spiritual, evangelicals leaned into old tropes about the spiritual-
ity of African Americans, while using them to promote interracialism based in religion, not rights.

Billy Graham deployed a similar strategy in his
revivals. Since the late 1950s, the events had included singer Ethel Waters, who went up to the
altar to dedicate her life to Christ in 1957 at Graham's Madison Square revival. The video recording of Waters at the Billy Graham Crusade in 1969
singing "Where Jesus Is, 'Tis Heaven" demonstrates
some interesting racial politics that helped Waters
connect with the crowd. Wearing a red dress with a
kerchief on her head, she started out by addressing
the crowd in a folksy way—"Hi! Bless your heart!"
She went on, "You know, babies, that's the way I
have to reach you. The Lord has been so good to
me this year. Just think, I was back in New York
this year, thanks to my precious baby Billy. Oh, I
just love that boy so." Here, she refers to the crowd
as her children in a performance of a kind of Black
motherhood and Black piety that was respectful,
familial, and, most important, unthreatening.

Performances of this sort, which I term performances of "Christian Blackness," were an accept-
able form of integration for evangelicals from the

1960s into the 1980s. Pious and reverent, they met white expectations and produced a cottage industry on the televangelist and evangelist circuit.

In addition to Ethel Waters, Billy Graham featured Grammy Award–winning singer Andraé Crouch at his revivals as well as sports figures like Rosey Grier. Grier, who followed up a career as a professional football player by becoming a bodyguard for Robert Kennedy, was known for having wrestled the gun away from Sirhan Sirhan immediately after Sirhan shot Kennedy. Later in his life, Eldridge Cleaver, formerly the Black Panther Party's minister of information, became a Christian and gained popularity on the evangelical circuit. Cleaver was baptized at Lake Arrowhead Springs in California, a popular site for evangelical camps. In a prominent *New York Times* article in 1977, Cleaver claimed that Billy Graham had called Cleaver's conversion "the second most important decision for Christ possible."

Following Oral Roberts's lead, televangelists across the nation began to integrate their television shows. Pat Robertson, who started the now popular Christian Broadcasting Network in Virginia, invited Ben Kinchlow to cohost his original show. Kinchlow became the show's affable African American sideman who often had to put up with Robertson's gaffes. In California, Jan and Paul Crouch, founders of the Trinity Broadcasting Network, drew from the network of Black pastors and gospel artists who had performed in Southern California at Anaheim's Melodyland to provide music and testimonials for their shows. As time passed, such integrated, interracial relationships as promoted by these evangelical leaders trickled down into what would be called the "megachurch movement" that began in the 1980s. Megachurches are large, predominantly suburban churches that usually have more than 2,000 members and multiple services daily. With the proliferation of evangelical megachurches in the South and Southern California— for example, Saddleback Church in Orange County, California, and John Osteen's church in Houston (John was Joel Osteen's father)—some congregations began to integrate slowly alongside evangelical Bible schools and seminaries.

These churches burgeoned during the Reagan era, and televangelist ministries rapidly grew. Jim and Tammy Faye Bakker through their *PTL Club*, Pat Robertson, and many others featured Black Christian luminaries on their shows to promote their own products and preaching engagements.

Then came the televangelist scandals of the late 1980s. Jim Bakker fell to sexual scandal. Jerry Falwell undertook a hostile takeover of Bakker's theme park and condo scheme, Heritage USA. Americans were treated to the spectacle of Jimmy Swaggart crying "I have sinned" after being caught trolling for sex workers. The proliferation and impact of these televangelists waned, and evangelicals were left wanting something new.

The end of the Reagan era and the subsequent presidential campaign of 1988, which pitted Republican sitting vice president George H. W. Bush against Democrat Michael Dukakis, signaled a shift in evangelical political action as the 1990s unrolled. Indeed, Bush faced an evangelical primary challenger: Pat Robertson, the owner of Christian Broadcasting Network. While Bush won the Republican nomination, Robertson did so well for a while as to come in second in the Iowa caucus.

It is safe to say that Republicans took notice. This is the moment when, leaving nothing on the table, Republican strategist and campaign advisor Lee Atwater deployed his infamous Willie Horton ad campaign against Democratic candidate Michael Dukakis. This was a baldly race-baiting TV production that featured Horton, a prisoner who had raped a white Maryland woman and bound and stabbed her boyfriend while on furlough during Dukakis's term as governor of Massachusetts. Using this ferociously racialized campaign against Dukakis had ramifications for years to come, both in general cultural perception and in the actual criminal justice policies of the 1990s. By playing to scurrilous images, dragged out of the nineteenth century, of Black men as beasts and rapists, and by simultaneously courting the evangelical vote, Bush was able to win the election. Atwater's Southern strategy worked.

Bush may have won the votes of the vast majority of evangelicals and the election, but his erstwhile opponent Pat Robertson a year later proceeded to found the immensely influential—and clearly politically directed—Christian Coalition. In October 1989, the Christian Coalition was created to help support grassroots political action by Christians—that is, evangelicals. Robertson wanted to capitalize on the enthusiasm he had seen on the campaign trail and to continue with the political tradition in which he had grown up, as his father, A. Willis Robertson, had served in the United States House and Senate and was also a segregationist. By this time, Robertson had already amassed a fortune in television, but now he wanted to participate in the political realm, and he wanted to invite other Christians at every level of society to do so as well.

The Christian Coalition, like many evangelical organizations of the day, was concerned with abortion, homosexuality, and other, as they saw it, moral issues, but it rocketed to success as a powerful lobbying arm under the control of Ralph Reed, who was hired as executive director in 1990. Reed, who was president of his College Republicans chapter, had spent his undergraduate years writing columns for the student newspaper about such topics as "Black genocide," decrying a high rate of abortions in the African American community. This angle was and continues to be an important strategy for evangelicals to reach out to churchgoing African Americans in order to bring them into supporting the pro-life position and into voting for conservative issues.

Through local chapters of the Christian Coalition, Reed established a powerful network of evangelical voters and lobbyists who, setting up dedicated offices in Washington, D.C., could phonebank and send faxes to the House and Senate on issues of evangelical concern.

Most important, they produced voter's guides that were openly distributed at churches across the nation. I should know. I got a couple in the run-up to the 1992 election.

The Christian Coalition did serious work to organize evangelical voters. Not only did their voter's guides give evangelicals a list of who to vote for to take with them to the polls, but the coalition also, according to historian Daniel K. Williams, presented evangelicals as a "persecuted minority." This was a key concept marking a key moment, as this way of thinking helped to transform the grassroots evangelicals trained by the Christian Coalition into a motivated, determined voting bloc.

With victories in local and statewide elections starting in 1990, the Christian Coalition began to align itself solidly with the Republican Party. In 1992, despite evangelicals' love for Republican primary candidate Pat Buchanan, the coalition backed

George H. W. Bush against Bill Clinton for president. Bush overtly accepted the coalition's help, putting himself squarely on their side in what sociologist James Davison Hunter called the "culture wars," as he titled his 1991 book.

"The culture wars" became *the* defining phrase for evangelicals in the 1990s, a decade that saw the Christian Coalition become a major force in pushing a moral- and social-issues-based agenda that opposed abortion and homosexuality and promoted conservatism. And African Americans were targeted as part of the coalition's plan. According to Daniel K. Williams, Ralph Reed made special efforts to reach out to Black Americans on educational and gay rights issues. This was part of a broad strategy to pursue stronger ties with African Americans *in spite of* the punishing, to Blacks, racial politics of the Reagan and Bush eras. Counterintuitively, perhaps, this strategy entailed efforts at racial reconciliation.

The racial reconciliation movements of the 1990s between white evangelicals and African Americans took several forms and met with varying degrees of success. Before the 1990s, an attempts at racial reconciliation often took the form of joint church services or days of visitation between churches. Occasionally, individuals would come out with apologies for previous racist behavior, including Jerry Falwell, who apologized for criticizing Martin Luther King Jr. —no matter that Falwell went on to oppose in 1983, along with Senator John McCain, the establishment of King's birthday as a national holiday. Much in keeping with evangelical theology, racism at that time was not considered a corporate sin—it was an individual sin. Even on that score, not many white evangelicals apologized for the racism that lurked in their hearts. Not until the 1990s did evangelicals begin to consider the possibility of a broader social culture of racism.

The change was noticeable over the course of the twentieth century's final decade. And one of the catalysts for the changing conversation came from a football coach. Another catalyst was a recorded police beating, which does not fail to reflect other horrifying images that continue to this day.

In 1990, then University of Colorado Boulder football coach Bill McCartney started a Christian men's group called Promise Keepers. Much of both positive and negative tinge has been written about Promise Keepers—envisioned by McCartney as a movement "for training and teaching on what it means to be godly men"—and evangelical men, but it is important to mark its founding as a moment that promoted racial reconciliation. By some measures, it was the first large and popular movement to do so. For McCartney, the drive for racial reconciliation came from his experiences as a football coach and the death of a former player on his team in the 1980s.

The crowd that attended McCartney's first

Promise Keepers meeting, which was designed to support men in small groups, was very white. Mc-Cartney felt that men did not want to be sermonized to about racial reconciliation. They wanted to roll up their sleeves, get in deep, and be in relationship. His approach focused not on the corporate and structural issues of racism but, as evangelicals were likely to see it, on individual relationships. Designed to be nonconfrontational on a structural level, Promise Keepers asked that participants deal with their own racial perceptions. One of the promises that the men were required to embrace was "A Promise Keeper is committed to reaching beyond any racial and denominational barriers to demonstrate the power of biblical unity."

Racial reconciliation efforts are chronicled by Andrea Smith in *Unreconciled: From Racial Reconciliation to Racial Justice in Christian Evangelicalism*. Looking at reconciliation work from the 1990s to the present, Smith rightfully states that such efforts tended to focus on multicultural representation in congregations and denominations rather than on structural forms of white supremacy. Much in keeping with Promise Keepers' and earlier evangelical understandings of racism as individual and not corporate sin, efforts to combat racism over the years have been about comfort, not about substantive change. This was apparent in the Los Angeles "Love LA" church efforts after the beating of Rodney King by Los Angeles police in 1991 after a high-speed chase in the San Fernando Valley.

The beating might not have become a worldwide phenomenon but for the invention of the video camera and for George Holliday's recording of the event, which he then sent to Los Angeles television station KTLA. The fifteen-minute-long beating was savage, leaving King with a cracked skull, broken teeth, and brain damage. Four officers were charged for the beating. In the trial about thirteen months later, all four were acquitted. Three hours later, on April 29, 1992, the city of Los Angeles erupted in flames. The uprising, or riots, depending on whose accounts one reads, was a defining moment for the city. In subsequent federal efforts to understand the LAPD response to the riots, major churches tried to reach across the divide. One of these churches was Church on the Way in Van Nuys, pastored by well-known Pentecostal pastor Jack Hayford.

Here is where evangelical racism intersects with my personal story. Once upon a time, I was an evangelical. A Pentecostal, to be exact. I was happily ensconced in Church on the Way and was preparing to start at Fuller Seminary in the fall of 1992. That spring, the Rodney King verdict came down and the riots happened. I had a front-row seat to one of the ways that evangelicals decided to deal with this traumatic event. Evangelical churches decided to come together under the aegis of Church on the Way's Pastor Hayford to hold what they called a "Love LA" service to heal the racial and social wounds of the city. Joining Hayford were Lloyd John Ogilvie of Hollywood Presbyterian Church and Kenneth Ulmer of Faithful Central Bible Church, a large African American church based in southern Los Angeles. It was to be a healing celebration, a chance for racial reconciliation.

For me, it was the moment I found out that despite my frenetic activity and full-steam participation in the church, I was invisible. For the service, I was sitting by Hayford's mother, who knew me from several other events. She turned to me at the greeting time and said, "Welcome to Church on the Way." At that moment, I knew that no matter how much I had worked or served or prayed with people, I was simply a Black person visiting the Church on the Way. Much like many evangelicals of color, I was just a Black person in this woman's white space. I had been welcomed due to the situation, but I couldn't possibly be a member of the church she belonged to. That moment encapsulated for me what evangelical attempts at interracial cooperation accomplished. Invisibility.

The Love LA event would go on to become a prayer group with more than 1,800 pastors participating for a few years afterward to pray for the city. The program was best summed up by Bryce Little, then pastor of mission and community outreach at

Hollywood Presbyterian. Quoted in *Christianity Today*, he observed, "Some feel prayer is not a program. We feel otherwise." Prayers, it seemed, would permeate most of the other major efforts at racial reconciliation in the 1990s. Pentecostals held their own racial reconciliation meeting in 1994. They called it "The Memphis Miracle." At the meeting, Black and white Pentecostals decided to dissolve the Pentecostal Fellowship of North America, an all-white Pentecostal organization, and created a new multiracial organization called the Pentecostal and Charismatic Churches of North America. The meeting was notable for a foot-washing service during which Bishop Charles Blake washed the feet of the Assemblies of God superintendent Thomas Trask. Trask then reciprocated. In a sense, this ceremony put Black people in the position of having to extend a symbol of racial reconciliation before the very perpetrators of anti-Blackness. While the meeting led to a structural change and a new organization, the event itself did not appreciably change the denomination's racial structure pattern.

The following year, during its 1995 annual convention, which coincided with the denomination's 150th anniversary, the Southern Baptist Convention issued an apology for slaveholding and racism. The Southern Baptist Convention wrote and then ratified a formal resolution condemning the group's role in slavery. I list here the crucial points from this resolution:

The resolution was designed as repentance and a plea for forgiveness for the sins of slavery and for the systemic racism in which the church had engaged. It intended, too, to chart a way forward toward racial reconciliation, and it was an important event for the Southern Baptist Convention. Richard Land, at the time head of the denomination's Christian Life Commission, was quoted in the *Atlanta Journal-Constitution* as saying that the resolution represented "movement toward the goal of a multi-racial, multi-ethnic denomination made up of churches that are open to everyone but give people an opportunity to express their own worship traditions."

Let us take a closer look at the resolution and Land's statement in light of the history of evangelicalism and racism. First, while it is commendable that the convention's statement acknowledges the role of slavery in how the Southern Baptist Convention was founded in the nineteenth century, it does not consider the theologies that were constructed around slaveholding or the perpetuation of those beliefs in the denomination. It does a great job at apologizing, but it does not address restitution for the structural racism within the denomination.

Perhaps the most telling quality of the resolution —and of Southern Baptist understandings of race and ethnicity—is Land's notion of moving toward a multiracial, multiethnic denomination open to everyone, along with "an opportunity [for them] to express their own worship traditions." In other words, everyone is welcome, and you can even play your Black gospel music. But this invitation ignores the much harder work of racial reconciliation that fosters a multicultural congregation, individual relationships among all kinds of people, and the modeling of togetherness through an appreciation of religious traditions. The resolution does not deal with the roots of racism that run deep within both the religious and the political positions of the denomination. Whether this approach, still common today, will be sustained by white evangelicals many decades after the beating of Rodney King and, more recently, after the murder of George Floyd by the knee of a Minneapolis police officer remains to be seen. A reckoning is on the near horizon.

We've seen how, from the sixties through the nineties, evangelicals had to confront issues of racism in an acute way. Criticisms confronted them within their ranks from fellow African American worshippers. Criticisms also hit them from African Americans outside of white evangelical denominational and social constructs. But my point is that, even while white evangelicals may have begun to change their social attitudes and habits in order to accommodate African Americans in churches and schools, in the political realm white evangelicals supported candidates and positions that were unremittingly conservative and designed to keep

African Americans and other ethnic groups out of positions of power.

During this era, evangelicals consolidated power both by aligning themselves with the Republican Party and by taking on a moral mantle that showed off their strong stances against abortion and homosexuality. Indeed, these were the two issues that would allow them to build their power through organizing and fundraising and that would, more and more, allow them to align themselves with electoral, and presidential, power. These issues would definitely increase their visibility in the media while proving to sustain a formidable fundraising machine that would provide means for white leaders, almost always male with the exception of Phyllis Schlafly. Through these means, they would build organizations like Focus on the Family and the Eagle Forum to energetically promote evangelical concerns and values . . . from a perspective of white hegemony.

While evangelical overtures toward racial reconciliation were numerous, the results were short-lived and cosmetic at best. The new millennium however, would challenge evangelicals and fundamentally change their orientation to both themselves and the public in striking, and dangerous, ways.

4

HOW FIRM A FOUNDATION

A Twenty-First-Century Precipice Appears

As we have seen in this trip through American history, racism consistently figured in the very structures of American evangelical life. Over the course of the twentieth century, racism persisted as poisonously as ever, though evangelical leaders learned how to deploy it covertly when they wanted to. Evangelical visions of political power would become a reality in the twenty-first century but came at the expense of the shield of morality that cloaked their ambitions. This vision and the activism that accompanied it have come at great expense to evangelicals.

By 2000, evangelicals allowed, seemingly without ambivalence, their traditional religiosity and moralism to become yoked to national electoral politics, and the structural racism in evangelicalism clearly and visibly exploded. The very first year of the new century saw George W. Bush run against John McCain to secure the Republican nomination for president of the United States. When Bush began to lag in the polls in South Carolina—a stronghold of white evangelical voters—flyers and push polls began appearing in that state blatantly accusing, or implicitly suggesting, that McCain's adopted daughter from Bangladesh was really a Black child he fathered out of wedlock. Just one year later, the horrible events of 9/11 saw the intense racialization of Islam and concomitant Islamophobia burst open. While these developments were in no way limited to evangelicals, Franklin Graham, eldest son of the very twentieth-century Billy Graham, famously called Islam "a very evil and wicked religion." And, still in the early years of the new century, racism became an undeniable aspect of American evangelicalism and evangelicals' public persona, given their racially charged opposition to candidate and then president Barack Obama, their seduction by Donald Trump's birtherism, and their full-on embrace of President Trump.

Up to this time, evangelicals had cloaked themselves in morality, respectability, and power. Their politics seemed, to the average onlooker, and per-

George W. Bush, who without one beat of hesitation said, "Christ . . . because he changed my heart." This was the 2000 election campaign's "Christ Moment," proclaimed the *Washington Post*'s December 16, 1999, edition. Bush's response thrilled evangelicals, but it made others suspicious. When asked by an Iowa reporter to clarify his answer, Bush backed off from his statement, saying he hadn't quite understood the question. Nevertheless, evangelicals began to turn toward him with interest. Bush would become the favorite candidate of evangelicals—but his presidential story represented the evangelical world with regard to race.

According to Daniel K. Williams, the Bush campaign balanced an inclusive language of compassion against the more polarizing aspects of the religious right. This was no accident, as Bush understood how to appeal to evangelicals: not from a distance but up close and personal. He had worked extensively with evangelicals during his father's failed reelection campaign in 1992, and he had plenty of connections in their world. In fact, the younger Bush improved upon his father's relationship with evangelicals while using the same type of tactical racism that his father had used in the 1988 Willie Horton campaign—just with a lighter touch. When Bush arrived in South Carolina to campaign on February 2, 2000, things looked bad for him. He'd lost much of his fifty-point lead on Senator John McCain, who defeated him by nineteen points in the New Hampshire primary. One respected, unnamed religious-right leader explained what happened next to a *Vanity Fair* reporter, who published an article titled "The Trashing of John McCain" after the election: "I always knew that if Bush got in trouble, he'd push the doomsday button."

The "doomsday button" involved two separate steps. The first was a campaign stop at Bob Jones University—a signal to South Carolina evangelicals that Bush believed like one of them. Bob Jones University was an integral part of Greenville, despite not having regained its tax-exempt status. Bush's appearance met with a warm welcome of over 6,000 enthusiastic people. The inevitable backlash to his visit to the university was plastered all over the mainstream media. Appearing on *Meet the Press* the following week, Bush renounced the university's position on interracial dating—but it was, as they say, easier to ask forgiveness than to ask permission.

The visit paid off for Bush in many ways, but it was Ralph Reed's pledge to Karl Rove that he could deliver in South Carolina that spurred on the full-court press against McCain. Rove, a Republican political strategist who worked for both George H. W. Bush and his son, knew the kinds of tactics that the Bush family had previously employed with regard to race. South Carolina, a stronghold of Reed's Christian Coalition, was ripe for a racialized smear campaign geared toward evangelicals. Richard Gooding wrote in *Vanity Fair* that it was an underground campaign modeled on Reed's dramatic statement about his Christian Coalition work: "I paint my face and travel at night. You don't know it's over until you're in a body bag. You don't know until Election Night." The campaign came at John McCain through a professor at Bob Jones University, Richard Hand, who sent out an unsolicited email that supposedly summarized McCain's life story, accusing him of partying, drinking, womanizing, and siring a child out of wedlock. Hand wrote at the top of the email, "Please feel free to copy and/or send it to others." In a CNN interview, Hand was asked if it was okay to spread rumors about McCain having children out of wedlock. Hand replied, "I didn't spread. I responded to people that want to know why do you feel the way you do about the man's character."

The email traveled far, and flyers started to appear in mailboxes and on windshields talking about McCain's illegitimate Black child. In fact, the child in question was neither illegitimate nor Black; she was McCain's daughter Bridget, whom his wife, Cindy, had adopted after visiting a relief mission in Bangladesh. Nonetheless, rumors multiplied that Cindy McCain was a drug addict, that John McCain had contracted a venereal disease. It was brutal. While McCain struggled to recover from all the hits, he made the mistake of committing what to South Carolinians was sacrilege when he called the Confederate flag a symbol of racism and slavery. That helped the NAACP, which launched an economic boycott of the state around the same time, but it created more trouble for McCain's campaign. Bush ended up winning the state by eleven points. Soon after the primary, Bob Jones University changed its policy and began to allow interracial dating on campus.

In retrospect, the attack on McCain says much about the marriage between the Republican Party and evangelicals in the twenty-first century. While Billy Graham had once sought relationships with presidents, now political operatives, evangelical political action groups, lobbyists, and a cable and radio media empire all came together to support the candidates most likely to defend evangelical programs. It also showed just how much race—despite the racial reconciliation efforts of the 1990s—remained not only a problem but also a political tool evangelicals willingly wielded to win races, smear candidates, and shore up their base. Bush eventually became president of the United States after a hotly contested Florida election whose outcome was decided by the Supreme Court. His two terms had several defining moments in terms of race, the most important of which occurred in the aftermath of 9/11 and of Hurricane Katrina.

The 9/11 attack opened up a national wound. Evangelical wrestling with Islam dates back to the nineteenth century, but it was only at the end of the twentieth and the beginning of the twenty-first century that it took on the character of a sustained phobia. Evangelical missionaries were always interested in converting Muslims to Christianity. In 1990 missions strategist Luis Bush coined the term "10/40 window" to refer to the countries between 10 degrees north and 40 degrees north latitude, where a majority of the world's Muslims, Hindus, and Buddhists live, and the region became an urgent missions imperative for some evangelical organizations. After 9/11, the 10/40 window became one of the talking points of Islamophobic religious leaders. Evangelical leaders began to promote their subcultural identity, especially in light of the frequent post-9/11 reminders in the media from the president and others that "Islam is a religion of peace." The language of spiritual warfare had entered the parlance of evangelicals, especially those from the Pentecostal and charismatic traditions. It was beginning to push the traditional boundaries of evangelical churches toward a more Pentecostal style of worship, where policy and people believed to be "satanically influenced" or "of the devil" were denounced.

In the days immediately after the 9/11 attack, two prominent evangelicals provided a tried-and-true explanation for the tragedy: Americans had become too morally liberal and had fallen away from God. Appearing on *The 700 Club* to talk with

Pat Robertson, Jerry Falwell started in on the reasons why he believed the attack had happened: "Throwing God out successfully with the help of the federal court system, throwing God out of the public square, out of the schools, the abortionists have got to bear some burden for this because God will not be mocked. And when we destroy 40 million little innocent babies, we make God mad." Falwell railed against "the pagans and the abortionists and the feminists and the gays and the lesbians who are actively trying to make that an alternative lifestyle, the ACLU, People for the American Way," all of whom had "tried to secularize America." He concluded, "I point the finger in their face and say, 'You helped this happen.'" Robertson responded, "Well, I totally concur."

Falwell's invocation of the failure of the nation to follow evangelical morality might have played well to his constituency, but the raw wound of 9/11 provoked a massive public outcry against the two men. Falwell was forced to walk back his remarks, but the damage was already done. The statements, while ludicrous, fit right into the evangelical worldview of sin, suffering, and apocalyptic ends. President Bush, the most evangelical president to date, did not buy into this line of thinking. "The president believes that terrorists are responsible for these acts," said a White House spokesman. "He does not share those views and believes that those remarks are inappropriate." Yet, despite Falwell's horrible statement, he was at the National Cathedral at the president's invitation for the service of remembrance of the 9/11 victims. Regardless of how he felt about what Falwell had said, Bush could not fail to extend an invitation to one of the biggest evangelical political leaders in the nation.

I call Falwell's method of using a great tragedy as a way to signal the loss of morality of the nation or of individuals "evangelical hostage taking." By making these kinds of statements to ascribe blame to groups they deem "sinful" or lacking morality, evangelicals draw their followers closer to them while at the same time broadcasting their issues loud and clear. Although they may later apologize, their messages have already been broadcast and drawn attention from the press, giving evangelical concerns the maximum amount of media coverage. Evangelical hostage taking has racial overtones as well. It upholds white Christian morality as the gold standard for living, while blaming anything antithetical to evangelical beliefs about sex, morality, and capitalism for the existence of suffering, death, and pain. In the case of Falwell's and Robertson's statements, not only were "liberal" policies to blame but Islam and Muslims as well—and this was only the beginning of evangelicals' shift to focusing their ire on Islam and Muslims in the post-9/11 world.

Bush fueled this ire with his use of the word "crusade" to describe the upcoming "War on Terror" to the American public post-9/11. The use of the word "crusade" in the context of an armed response to the Al Qaeda attack resonated with evangelicals' apocalyptic beliefs as well as their belief in the discounted but often cited "clash of civilizations" thesis of Samuel Huntington. Huntington argued that in the post–Cold War era, religious and cultural conflicts would be the primary sources of tension in the world. Bush's use of the language of crusade and his juxtaposition of a good America against an evil Iraq and Al Qaeda set up binaries that resonated with evangelicals, encouraging them not only to speak of Islam disparagingly but also to deepen their faith's embrace of nationalism and American exceptionalism. No surprise, then, that evangelicals began to refer to Islam in disparaging ways. At the Southern Baptist Convention in 2002, Rev. Jerry Vines, former president of the Southern Baptist Convention, said of the Prophet Muhammad that he was a demon-possessed pedophile whose twelfth and final wife was a nine-year-old girl. Vines also declared that Muslims worshipped a different God than Christians. President Bush, who spoke to the convention the day after Vines, made no reference to Vines's speech at all. Both Muslims and Christians condemned Vines's remarks, but his was only one in a rapid succession of disparaging speeches and sermons about Islam in the months following the 9/11 attacks.

While continuing to pit themselves against moral issues like same-sex marriage and abortion, evangelicals built an even greater disdain for Islam after 9/11. For some, this disdain became a reason to harass and murder. Franklin Graham called Islam "a very wicked and evil religion" after an interview on NBC's *Nightly News* in November 2001. Whole new cottage industries arose, including publishing anti-Islam books and stories of Muslim conversion to Christianity. While much of the racialization of Islam would occur later, following the election of Barack Obama to the presidency in 2008, the seeds of that racialization began after 9/11 with attacks on people who "looked" Muslim. The murder of Balbir Singh Sodhi by Frank Roque in Arizona days after 9/11 provides one example. Roque was upset in the wake of the 9/11 attacks and said to an Applebee's waiter, "I'm going to go out and shoot some towelheads." Four days later, he shot Sodhi five times in the back as Sodhi planted flowers at his gas station. Roque went on to shoot at a Lebanese man at another gas station, then to shoot up his previous home, which had been sold to an Arab family. When arrested, he shouted, "I am a patriot! I stand for America!"

Sodhi was not a Muslim—he was a Sikh. In the days following 9/11 and continuing even today, Sikh people, Arabic speakers, and other persons who appear to be "Muslim" are targeted by zealots eager to confront what they believe are radical terrorists living in their midst. This racialization through phenotype and dress became a regular connected in some way?" Dwight McKissic, pastor of Cornerstone Baptist Church in Arlington, Texas, remarked, "New Orleans flaunts its sin in a way that no other places do. . . . They have a southern Decadence parade every year and they call it gay pride. . . . They openly practice voodoo and devil worship. You can't shake your fist in God's face 364 days a year and then ask 'Where was God when Katrina struck?'" Of course, Franklin Graham also chimed in: "There's been satanic worship in New Orleans. There's been sexual perversion. God is going to use that storm to bring a revival. God has a plan. God has a purpose." Is it strange that no one blamed the catastrophe on the fact that New Orleans had been a major port for the original American sin, the transatlantic slave trade? But I digress.

Evangelical responses to Katrina were mixed, but these pronouncements and many others bracketed President Bush's horrible response to the natural disaster, which was slow, poorly coordinated, and racially insensitive. Between the evangelical denouncements, Bush's heartless flyover of New Orleans in Air Force One to view the devastation, and his disastrous photo op in front of St. Louis Cathedral lit up like Disneyland's castle, the unfeeling intransigence and racism of evangelicals was a cruel abomination. It took rapper Kanye West, during a telethon to raise money for Katrina survivors, to articulate what many Black people felt: "George Bush doesn't care about Black people." Bush later called this the lowest point of his presidency, though West apologized for the comment. The fact remained that Bush's inadequate response to the impending disaster and his stupid statements to the then director of FEMA Michael D. Brown, such as "Brownie, you're doing a heck of a job" when Black bodies were found in attics in the Ninth Ward, smacked of ignorance and blithe neglect.

Evangelicals' political, moral, and theological concerns had come together to create a harsh, uncaring posture toward suffering and disaster. Rather than seeing events like 9/11 or Katrina as man-made murders or natural disasters, they chose to blame the dead, dying, and suffering for moral infractions that violated deeply held evangelical beliefs. At the same time, evangelicals constantly referred to themselves as victims, a persecuted minority because of their faith. These contradictions, and this strategy of evangelicals to use morality as a cudgel to mask racism, became a regular feature of the Bush era and beyond, setting the stage for the much more virulent, in-your-face racism of the 2008 election and its aftermath.

The 2008 presidential election represents a turning point in the story of evangelical racism. It marked the first time the United States had an African American Democratic candidate for president, Barack Hussein Obama. The election launched a new class of evangelical power brokers: Pentecostals and charismatics who embodied much of the racial politics of evangelicalism and aggrieved evangelical leaders like Franklin Graham, Robert Jeffress, and others who articulated a more radical message of morality through race and racism. Finally, it was a woman, Sarah Palin, John McCain's running mate, who clearly set out a refreshed version of evangelical morality politics—the politics of grievance, racial resentment, and American exceptionalism. Palin harnessed the seething resentments that grew throughout the campaign season, making public the racism that had long been festering right beneath the surface of evangelical life. Most important, she created the blueprint for the 2016 presidential campaign and a whole cottage industry of right-wing media, which evangelicals capitalized on.

John McCain was not evangelicals' first choice for their 2008 candidate. Former senator Fred Thompson, who did not win a single primary, and Mike Huckabee, the governor of Arkansas, were leading contenders. Neither could pull out the wins they needed, however, and McCain became the nominee over the protests of evangelical leaders like James Dobson, who did not care for him. McCain had to resort to trying to get those on the margins of the evangelical world to support him, namely John Hagee, a Texas pastor and the founder of Christians United for Israel (CUFI), and Rod Parsley, a bombastic charismatic megachurch pastor from Ohio. Both ended up being jettisoned from the McCain campaign: Hagee because he said "their God sent a hunter" in Hitler to fulfill biblical prophecy, and Parsley after he called Islam "inherently violent" and an "anti-Christ" religion. Meanwhile, Obama had his own pastor problems. The Reverend Dr. Jeremiah Wright, his pastor in Chicago, gave a sermon in which he invoked a jeremiad, saying, "God damn America." Fox News replayed the sermon ad nauseam, and it followed Obama throughout the campaign. In the wake of the furor over Wright's sermon, Obama gave a race speech in Philadelphia on March 18, 2008—notable for being the first speech of its kind given by a presidential candidate—in which he attempted to deal with Wright's characterization of America, his own Christian belief, and the racism of the campaign. While the speech was lofty and enlightening, it betrayed Obama's weak spot: he always believed that his opponents would rise to the occasion rather than sink to the depths of racial animus.

Obama's naïve belief that Republicans, and evangelicals by default, would play fair was a major miscalculation on his part—not just in the campaign but in his presidency. By March 2008, questions were already being raised about Obama having studied at a madrassa as a youth in Indonesia, and rumors were circulating about him not being an American citizen. These rumors eventually morphed into the "birtherism" campaign, which claimed that Obama was a Muslim and was not an

American citizen because his father was Kenyan. By August 2008, meanwhile, McCain's people had tried every way they could think of to get the religious right on board with his campaign, even creating a commercial called "The One" that insinuated Barack Obama was the Antichrist. The brainchild of Fred Davis, who was a close friend of Ralph Reed, head of the Christian Coalition, the commercial showed Obama as a sinister figure, à la the *Left Behind* series. The ad opens with an ominous voice saying, "It should be known that in 2008 the world shall be blessed. They will call him THE ONE." The ad goes on to show Obama as a megalomaniacal figure who promises to heal the world, uttering the phrase "We are the ones we've been waiting for." With its ominous language, the tone of the ad was designed to invoke and play on the apocalyptic beliefs of evangelicals. At the same time, rumors that Obama was not American but Kenyan and a Muslim were making the rounds in email chains and on right-wing conspiracy websites.

Ultimately, though, it was not racist ads or rumormongering but McCain's selection of Governor Sarah Palin of Alaska as his vice-presidential running mate that won evangelicals over to McCain. Born Catholic, Palin was raised in the Assemblies of God (Pentecostal) faith. She attended a nondenominational church in Wasilla, Alaska, and was mother of five, including Trig, a child with Down syndrome who was not yet one year old. Pretty, charismatic, and a gun-toting Christian, Palin seemed like just the person to spice up the campaign—and please evangelicals. The news that McCain had chosen her as his running mate was met with tremendous enthusiasm in the evangelical community. James Dobson from Focus on the Family expressed it clearly: "A lot of people were praying, and I believe Sarah Palin is God's answer. Sen. McCain has chosen a solid conservative who has a reputation for espousing common sense. Gov. Palin's commitment to the sanctity of life is not just a political position. She was advised to abort her fifth and youngest child when it was learned he had Down Syndrome. She refused. That's bravery and integrity in action." Phyllis Schlafly told *WorldNetDaily*, a conservative Christian magazine, that McCain's choice of Palin was "the best he could possibly have made." Palin had "reinvigorated the entire Republican Party," Schlafly said. "And it's across the board. It's not just pro-lifers. She's a breath of fresh air. She's right on every issue." The foot soldiers of the right recognized Palin as one of their own. Emails poured into the governor's office in Alaska with congratulations and promises to pray for her. The elation, however, soon changed to surprise. Before Palin could even give a speech at the Republican National Convention, evangelicals were taken aback by the news of Palin's daughter Bristol's out-of-wedlock pregnancy. Excuses were conveniently made, and the news was shared that Bristol and her boyfriend, pallin' around with terrorists who would target their own country." The response was electric. Palin had skillfully tacked away from criticisms of her performance toward incendiary statements about Obama. Her reference to Obama not seeing America as "you and I" do tapped into a deep well of nationalistic racial pride.

Palin's speech became a defining one for her populist messaging on the campaign trail, and it resonated with the racial animus of some of the people who thronged to see her. With her speech at the Republican National Convention, in which she quoted deceased journalist Westbrook Pegler on "small towns," Palin began to make a populist, racialized turn—one that brought out the pitchforks. She neatly folded all of the rumors about Obama into a nice package in which he was the "Manchurian candidate," a crypto-Muslim who had studied at a radical madrassa in Indonesia and who wasn't born in America.

Palin's stump speeches became racist, nationalistic rallies. Supporters yelled out words like "terrorist," "treason," and "kill him!" as she repeatedly used the "Obama's pallin' around with terrorists" line. The media did not know what to do with this new turn of events. Some were dumbfounded; others criticized the campaign heavily for this new tactic. Reporters for Al Jazeera, attending a McCain-Palin rally in St. Clairsville, Ohio, were dumbfounded by Palin's responses to questions

117

about Obama, such as "I'm afraid if he wins, the Blacks will take over. He's not a Christian! This is a Christian nation! What is our country gonna end up like?" or "When you got a Negra running for president, you need a first-stringer. He's definitely a second-stringer." The Secret Service even began to investigate the rallies, fearful of the violence that Palin was provoking on the trail. McCain contributed to the poisonous environment by asking, "Who is the real Barack Obama?" and feigning dismay when John Lewis compared the rallies to the worst of Bull Connor in the civil rights movement.

Palin pushed the socialist, communist, and terrorist misconceptions about Obama by cultivating dog whistles, including the terms "small towns," "real America," and "pro-America," into a powerful, pungent mix of Christian populist and patriotic racism that delineated who was "one of us"—that is, a God-fearing Christian, white, and pro-America. While the mainstream media thought her inept, Palin was shrewd in her calls to American exceptionalism and nationalism. By evoking nostalgia for the "good old days" of small towns and apple pie, Palin tugged at the heartstrings of older white evangelicals who did not want to see a Black man in the White House. Moreover, she did this when the McCain campaign had fallen behind in the polls after the September 2008 financial crash—cause for alarm among evangelical leadership. *Charisma* magazine publisher Stephen Strang claimed, "Life as we know it will end if Obama is elected."

Donald Wildmon of the American Family Association sent out a fundraising letter that warned, "This country that we love, founded on Judeo-Christian values, will cease to exist and will be replaced by a secular state hostile to Christianity. This 'city set on a hill' which our forefathers founded, will go dark." No kidding. The darkness of Obama's skin was what they believed would cause the country to go dark. Dobson's Focus on the Family even sent out a twelve-page "Letter from 2012 in Obama's America," which outlined what would happen if Obama were to become president. The beginning of the letter was a tour de farce of evangelical schmaltz:

I can hardly sing "The Star Spangled Banner" any more. When I hear the words,

O say, does that star-spangled banner yet wave
O'er the land of the free and the home of the brave?

I get tears in my eyes and a lump in my throat. Now in October of 2012, after seeing what has happened in the last four years, I don't think I can still answer, "Yes," to that question. We are not "the land of the free and the home of the brave." Many of our freedoms have been taken away by a liberal Supreme Court and a Democratic majority in both the House and the Senate, and hardly any brave citizen dares to resist the new government policies any more.

The letter went on to predict the appointment of liberal Supreme Court justices, that the Supreme Court would declare same-sex marriage a constitutional right, and that the Boy Scouts would have to hire homosexual scoutmasters and allow them to sleep in tents with young boys.

Dobson's imagination offered insight into the fearmongering and incitement happening in evangelical circles alongside the decline of McCain and Palin in the polls. Evangelicals were so fearful of an Obama win that conservative right-wing evangelicals piled on about Obama. Day Gardner, president of the National Black Pro-Life Union, put out a press release challenging Obama's Christianity because of his pro-choice stance: "Obama says he is a Christian, yet he supports abortion, all abortion! . . . So what God does Obama worship? What kind of Christian would openly and purposefully go against the Bible, the word of God? Maybe one who is not a Christian at all!"

Thus the 2008 election cycle marked a new juncture in evangelicalism and racism. The election of Barack Obama was a sign of the apocalypse for evangelicals. Because of the marriage of evangelical morality to the Republican Party—all in the service of maintaining white conservative male leadership—the election signaled a failure of the evangelical political machine. It also stripped the gloves off the carefully crafted racial reconciliations of the 1990s and moved evangelicals toward an alliance with outwardly racist movements. Evangelicals found themselves making friends with strange but like-minded conspirators who promoted their ideologies and took them down a path toward embracing openly racist memes and themes to get their messages out.

The most important of these new friends was the Tea Party. Birthed in the heart of capitalism, the new evangelical partner did not originate from the pulpit but from a fiscal evangelist on a trading floor. On February 19, 2009, Rick Santelli, an on-air personality at CNBC, made a rant from the floor of the Chicago Mercantile Exchange that would bring about a new political movement. Asked to comment on President Obama's plan to shore up underwater mortgages, Santelli said, "The government is promoting bad behavior!" He trashed the plan: "How many of you people want to pay for your neighbor's mortgage that has an extra bathroom and can't pay their bills? Raise your hand!" No hands were raised. Chants of "no" arose around him, and then Santelli said in exasperation, "We're thinking of having a Chicago tea party in July! All you capitalists that wanna show up to Lake Michigan, I'm gonna start organizing!"

Looking back, Santelli's speech is telling, for in it lie seeds of religiosity that sound like the prosperity gospel—the belief that God wants you to be rich, and if you pay your tithes and offerings and believe, God will bless you abundantly. "Bad behavior" is code for immorality, and equating fiscal responsibility with morality was a move that resonated strongly with evangelicals, for whom this language was part of their history. Many evangelicals share beliefs of capitalism, the founding of America, and the idea that wealth is a blessing. Santelli's message rallied not only fiscal conservatives but evangelicals as well. His rant became the founding moment of the Tea Party, defined by political scientists Theda Skocpol and Vanessa Williamson as a movement of "grassroots activists, roving billionaire advocates, and right-wing media purveyors [who create] the Tea Party and give it the ongoing clout to buffet and redirect the Republican Party and influence broader debates in American democracy." The Pew Forum on Religion and Public Life conducted a survey on the Tea Party in February of 2011. It found that "Tea Party supporters tend to have conservative opinions not just about economic matters, but also about social issues such as abortion and same-sex marriage. In addition, they are more likely than registered voters as a whole to say that their religion is the most important factor in determining their opinions on these social issues. And they draw disproportionate support from the ranks of white evangelical Protestants."

David Brody, correspondent on the Christian Broadcasting Network, called evangelical or Christian supporters of the Tea Party "Teavangelicals" in order to separate them out from the regular Tea Party members. It is worth unpacking Brody's term, because it gets at the downward spiral of evangelical racial politics. Teavangelicals believe that God, not government, is the first authority they should answer to. Criticizing government spending on the poor and government entitlements is one of the ways they make racist arguments without using racist language. Words like "poor" and "entitlement" are used to describe people of color, especially African Americans, as lazy and unwilling to work. This neatly dovetails with the Weberian "Protestant ethic" that many evangelicals espouse, an ethic of hard work, thrift, and a belief in capitalism and free markets. As Kevin Kruse points out in his book *One Nation under God: How Corporate America Invented Christian America*, capitalism and Christianity in America melded with free enterprise in the twentieth century. This affinity created an interesting synergy in the twenty-first century, supplanting the values of caring for the poor and the indigent with the values of free markets, individual responsibility, and a sense that the government should not provide assistance to those whom Teavangelicals viewed as unable to manage in the marketplace, whatever the reasons might be. This shift also made room for the charismatic and Pentecostal wings of evangelicalism, which believed in the prosperity gospel. This belief explains why, in part, Teavangelicals and some evangelicals have opposed health care reform: they believe that if you are blessed by God, God will provide for you.

The shift in evangelicals' relationship to both capitalism and government was in process prior to the Tea Party, but the Tea Party movement accelerated it. Not only was the Tea Party about money, but it also was a space in which evangelicals could express all of their grievances and the racial animus that had festered during the 2008 election cycle and magnify these feelings within a movement that cast them as "real Americans and patriots." Evangelicals' alliance with the Tea Party positioned them as arbiters of fiscal policy and of how that fiscal policy should affect their communities and the nation. Most troubling, it gave license to the racism, "birtherism," and Islamophobia that arose during the election cycle. All of this was amplified by those right-wing media purveyors who, with Facebook, Twitter, blogs, and news outlets, became the town criers of the movement.

The Tea Party movement and its raucous rallies, where participants dressed up in tricorn hats, became hotbeds for racist grievance. Posters displayed signs depicting President Obama as a witch doctor with the caption "Obamacare," and others read "Obama's plan is white slavery," "We don't need a Kenyan Marxist," and "Monkey see, monkey do." Sarah Palin became one of the movement's darlings, and Tea Partiers helped figures like Palin and Glenn Beck gain traction on the political scene in 2009–10.

Beck, a former alcoholic, radio personality, and Mormon convert, dominated the Fox airwaves from 2009 until 2011 with his show, *Glenn Beck.* It featured a prominent chalkboard with much scribbling and a series of guests designed to teach Fox viewers about the latest conspiracy theories, the evils of socialism, and the dangers of academics such as Frances Fox Piven and philanthropist George Soros. Beck was a modern-day Joseph McCarthy, hunting after anything that smelled of "un-Americanism," including Black theology. Beck also promoted weird apocalyptic theories that were a combination of right-wing fears and his own mind. Though his star began to wane in 2011 when he proposed that the Arab Spring was about a "caliphate" being set up in the Middle East, his media footprint in 2010 was formidable. Not only did he occupy the 5–6 P.M. EST time slot on Fox, but he also had a daily radio show and ran a popular website.

Tea Partiers were a natural demographic for Beck, who partnered with Sarah Palin for his 2010 Taking Our Country Back tour, designed to rally

Tea Partiers to demand a smaller government that adhered to the principles of the Founding Fathers. Both Palin and Beck, in their roles as America's evangelists of the right, promoted a pseudoreligion of guns, God, and flag that closely resembled dominionism, a type of fascist, neo-Christian framework that made the Bible not merely a Christian document but the very constitution of America. In spreading the message that the providence of God was in abeyance because of the election of Barack Obama, both Palin and Beck positioned themselves as political evangelists of the nation and "saviors" who could help rid America of President Obama in the next election cycle. What Beck did well was rally Tea Partiers on a national scale.

Beck's first big rally was the 9/12 protest in 2009, where he managed to gather local, state, and national Tea Party groups to march against President Obama's plan to reform health care. Palin's comments about "death panels" had helped to galvanize the group, and conservative funders like the Koch brothers provided the money and commercials that recruited Tea Party patriots. A crowd of about 70,000 hit Washington, D.C., with some signs depicting President Obama as Hitler and the Antichrist and others bearing the slogan "Bury Obamacare with Kennedy"—a reference to Senator Ted Kennedy, who had recently passed away. The event was notable for its racial undertones. Few African Americans attended, and the crowd's signs peculiar practice that was becoming prevalent with evangelicals and Republicans: the appropriation of Martin Luther King Jr.'s memory not only in the service of a color-blind gospel but as a promoter of evangelical and Republican moral values. King's statement from the "I Have a Dream" speech of 1963, "I have a dream that my four little children will one day live in a nation where they will not be judged by the color of their skin, but by the content of their character," was appropriated as a way to promote values of self-sufficiency and character, avoiding any conversations about race. Beck's use of the March on Washington imagery, then, was also about giving a sense of "righteousness" to the Tea Party movement, even as its followers embraced racist imagery to protest President Obama. It was no surprise, then, that the rally included gospel singers and Alveda King, a prominent Black conservative who is the niece of Dr. King.

Beck's remarks to the Tea Party group Freedom-Works indicated that the rally was religious, not political. "My role, as I see it, is to wake America up to the backsliding of principles and values and, most of all, God. We are a country of God. As I look at the problems in our country, quite honestly, I think the hot breath of destruction is breathing on our necks, and to fix it politically is a figure I don't see anywhere." Beck's apocalyptic language resonated with the Tea Party "Teavangelicals" who had gathered to attend the rally. "We are fed up with ing in March 2011 and continuing until 2016. His statements, such as this one on Fox News on March 28, 2011, combined citizenship with Islamophobia: "He doesn't have a birth certificate, or if he does, there's something on that certificate that is very bad for him. Now, somebody told me—and I have no idea if this is bad for him or not, but perhaps it would be—that where it says 'religion,' it might have 'Muslim.' And if you're a Muslim, you don't change your religion, by the way." The innuendo by Graham, Trump, *WorldNetDaily*, and other conservative and evangelical media outlets permeated the airwaves until Obama released his long-form birth certificate. A few days later, a secret raid killed Osama bin Laden, architect of the 9/11 attacks.

All of this points to several of the major changes that occurred in evangelical attitudes toward racism. The election of President Obama resulted in a higher tolerance for conspiracy theories, hucksterism (Trump), and out-and-out grievances becoming part of the evangelical worldview and culture. Even though many younger evangelicals found themselves voting in 2008 and 2012 for Barack Obama, older evangelicals viewed him as a threat not only to their ideals of the presidency but also to existential beliefs about their white nationalistic Christianity that had been an essential part of messaging from both their denominations and their media leadership. As a result, the grievances increased, as well as the ire against Obama.

Evangelicals began to use the language of "religious freedom" as a way to exclude LGBTQ persons from civil rights and to lobby for special status in cases such as the Masterpiece Cakeshop case.

The Masterpiece Cakeshop case originated in Colorado, where two gay men asked the Masterpiece Cakeshop to bake their wedding cake. The cake shop refused because of the owner's opposition to same-sex marriage and homosexuality on religious grounds. The religious freedom argument is an old one, originating in the nineteenth century, when evangelicals used religious beliefs about race to separate their denominations and justify slavery. They went on to use those same arguments to prevent giving rights to African Americans, to women, and to gays and lesbians. As Tisa Wenger writes in *Religious Freedom: The Contested History of an American Ideal*, "If religious freedom trumps equality under the law, it provides a cover that actually encourages discrimination."

While evangelicals were fighting against President Obama—from spreading birtherism lies to promoting the Tea Party, aggressive rallies, and religious freedom as a means by which their beliefs could be imposed on the public—racial animus and racialized violence began to dominate the airwaves in other ways.

The killing of Trayvon Martin by George Zimmerman in February 2012 was the first of a wave of new killings of African Americans by police or white vigilantes that debilitated and angered the African American community. These killings drew a new generation of African American youth and other leadership to press for justice—efforts that rankled some evangelicals and energized others for change. The formation of Black Lives Matter in 2013 and the subsequent murder of Michael Brown in Ferguson, Missouri, brought protests and militarized police units into the streets. Evangelicals' calls for peace and their support of the police alienated Black evangelicals and other African Americans. Robert Jeffress, pastor of First Baptist Church in Dallas, remarked on the killing of Michael Brown in Ferguson: "We do our congregations no favor when we give them the illusion that they can sail through life without ever being treated unjustly or hurt deeply. Perhaps Michael Brown's death in Ferguson was unwarranted, or maybe police officer Darren Wilson is the true victim. We don't know all the facts yet. But what we can say with certainty is that every one of us will at some time experience injustice."

"Maybe Darren Wilson is the true victim"—imagine that. He's not dead, but he's somehow the true victim of a crime in which this twenty-eight-year-old police officer put six bullets into eighteen-year-old Michael Brown, ending his life. Jeffress's view, however, is one held by many evangelicals regarding those in authority, including police officers. More often than not, evangelicals tend to impugn those who have been killed by law enforcement as lawbreakers. A study done by the Barna Group showed that only 13 percent of white evangelicals support the Black Lives Matter movement, while 76 percent are inclined to say "all lives matter." By placing the blame on victims rather than perpetrators, evangelicals couple an idealized vision of law enforcement with scriptural admonitions.

Franklin Graham added salt to the wound in March 2015 with a Facebook comment about police violence that he based on the biblical admonitions of "submitting to your leaders and those in authority" in Hebrews 13:17: "Listen up—Blacks, Whites, Latinos, and everybody else. Most police shootings can be avoided. It comes down to respect for authority and obedience. If a police officer tells you to stop, you stop. If a police officer tells you to put your hands in the air, you put your hands in the air. If a police officer tells you to lay down face first with your hands behind your back, you lay down face first with your hands behind your back. It's as simple as that. Even if you think the police officer is wrong—YOU OBEY."

Even when Black Christians were killed, evangelicals' responses did not address racial injustice. In 2015, Dylann Roof attended the Wednesday evening Bible study for an hour at Emanuel AME Church in Charleston, South Carolina, before shooting nine members of the church, including the Reverend Clementa Pinckney, a member of the

South Carolina state senate and senior pastor of the church. After police captured Roof, they took him for a burger at Burger King before remanding him into custody. The shock of this event crushed African American Christians, and while many churches addressed the murders in their pulpits the following Sunday morning with prayer, evangelicals quickly tacked to focus on anything but the root cause of the shooting: racism.

Evangelicals used the language of religious persecution as an excuse for why Roof decided to go into a church and kill nine Black people, rather than focusing on the very clear racist ideas that influenced him. Black conservative pastor E. W. Jackson connected the attack to the hatred of Christians, and former senator Rick Santorum of Pennsylvania talked about the importance of prayer and framed the shooting as "an assault on religious liberty." Franklin Graham said: "There are real people out there who are organized to kill people based on religion and based on race. This guy's just whacked out. But it's 2015. There are people out there looking for Christians to kill." Evangelicals also spoke out against the Confederate flag after pictures began to circulate of Roof holding up the flag, the symbol of the South and its separation from the Union over slavery. Russell Moore, president of the Ethics and Religious Liberty Commission of the Southern Baptist Convention, wrote a blog post soon after the shooting called "The

Cross and the Confederate Flag" urging Christians who had allegiance to the flag to give it up. Even Franklin Graham joined in the chorus, invoking his great-grandfathers who had fought for the South under the Confederate flag: "Growing up, many people in the South flew the Confederate flag; but I believe that it's time for this flag to be set aside as a part of our history."

It would fall to a Black Christian woman, Bree Newsome, daughter of a longtime dean of the Howard University School of Divinity, to take down the Confederate flag at the statehouse in South Carolina. While praying and reciting scriptures on the morning of June 27, 2015, she climbed the flagpole and removed the flag, which was held to the pole not by a rope but by screws embedded into the pole. Reciting as she came down the pole, "The Lord is my light and my salvation; of whom shall I fear," Newsome was arrested immediately upon reaching the ground.

Even the massacre of nine Black Christians following a Bible study class was not enough to make American evangelicals face the fact that racism remained a major problem within their ranks. They looked to religiosity and symbolism to deflect scrutiny of their own shortcomings and historical failures with regard to the racism in their churches. This willful blindness would open the door for a man who would be revered by them despite all of his moral failings. Donald Trump, who won the

Republican primary against sixteen opponents and won the presidency in 2016, would become both the savior and the nadir of the evangelical movement in America. Their embrace of this thrice-married, casino-owning reality TV star would both give them new recognition in the Republican Party and destroy the image of morality and uprightness they had so carefully cultivated. Evangelicals' embrace of an unrepentant racist solidified the place of racism in the history of American evangelicalism. More than that, their embrace tore the covers off the anti-Black racism that had existed since the nineteenth century.

Given all of this, is evangelicalism dead?

CONCLUSION

Whom Will You Serve?

Evangelicals, you have a problem. That problem is racism.

After taking this journey through the history of American evangelicalism, I know why evangelicals overwhelmingly support conservative Republicans and right-wing political positions and why they supported—unwaveringly—Donald Trump and his administration. That is, I know the answer to the question obsessively pondered by the popular press, pundits, and even experts in the study of American religion: Why do people who identify as evangelicals vote over and over again for political figures who in speech and deed do not evince the Christian qualities that evangelicalism espouses?

My answer is that evangelicalism is not a simply religious group at all. Rather, it is a nationalistic political movement whose purpose is to support the hegemony of white Christian men over and against the flourishing of others.

To put it more baldly, evangelicalism is an Americanized Christianity born in the context of white Christian slaveholders. It sanctified and justified segregation, violence, and racial proscription. Slavery and racism permeate evangelicalism, and as much as evangelicals like to protest that they are color-blind, their theologies, cultures, and beliefs are anything but. Evangelicals have burrowed their identities into the infrastructure of Republican politics since Billy Graham's relationship with Republican president Dwight D. Eisenhower. Evangelicalism is a religion that has benefited and continues to benefit from racism on both an individual level and a structural level, always under the guise of morality and patriotic nationalism. Racism in evangelicalism is not only about individual sin. It's about the corporate sins of a religious movement that continues to believe itself good, and that good is predicated on whiteness and the proximity to power.

As an African American woman who once trained in an evangelical seminary, I don't say these things lightly. Some of my most significant intellectual training took place during my time in evangelical circles. I am grateful for it. I left evangelicalism in graduate school more than twenty years ago. I know both intellectually and emotionally how evangelicals think about the movement and how they protect it—which puts me at odds with the evangelical historians who claim that the 81 percent of evangelicals who voted for Donald Trump in 2016 aren't really evangelicals. THEY ARE. The historians just wish fervently that they weren't.

I am vexed by the constant hand-wringing of evangelical scholars and popular writers explaining away their racism or, at worst, not even considering race in their analysis. Their very omission of race continues to promote the supposition that evangelicalism reads "white." Progressive evangelicals, like Jim Wallis of Sojourners, have tried another explanation to save the movement. In October 2016, Wallis wrote in *USA Today* an op-ed titled "Evangelicals Aren't Who You Think," claiming that evangelicals were also people of color and liberal and that the press has made evangelicalism "white." I do not buy that explanation either. Whether ignoring race or hiding behind race, the evangelical whitewashing of race and racism does not work anymore.

Evangelicalism is at a precipice. It is no longer a movement to which American Christians look for a moral center. American evangelicalism lacks social, political, and spiritual effectiveness in the twenty-

CONCLUSION

first century. It has become a religion lodged within a political party. It is a religion that promotes issues of importance almost exclusively to white conservatives. Evangelicalism embraces racists and says that evangelicals' interests, and only theirs, are those most important for all American citizens. This is a movement that could have and should have moved on from its roots in nineteenth-century racism and slavery revealed in this book. Yet it has not. And that is due to the choices made by leaders and followers within the evangelical movement.

Why have evangelicals and their leadership made choices over and over again to embrace racism? Because it is what has allowed them to attain and hold political power. Power, whether they admit it or not, is what individual evangelical churches and organizations have always wanted. Evangelicals hold old resentments about being shut out of the power-broker positions mainline Protestants traditionally held in America. Evangelicals were not well-heeled Presbyterians or Episcopalians. They could barely call themselves white Anglo-Saxon Protestants before the rise of Billy Graham. They longed for the institutions and prestige that the tall-steeple-church pastors had.

What evangelicals did have was whiteness, and whiteness eventually gave them power, social and political. When I say "whiteness," I know that evangelicals are not only white people; they also encompass many ethnic and racial groups. But

the prohibitions against interracial marriage on biblical grounds, and the belief that Christianity is "white" lead to a kind of thinking that unfortunately declares equality in the "gospel" but in practice is not the kind of equality that leads to respect, leadership, or appreciation of other cultures and religions. Recent articles about Black evangelical struggles with white evangelicals regarding race illuminate this issue painfully. Daniel Burke, a CNN religion correspondent, reported on this in an interview with Trillia Newbell, a Black Christian author. After she gave a talk about all people being in the Image of God, or the Imago Dei, a white man approached Newbell, telling her that "she was subhuman, and a different species" and even wanted to use scripture to prove it to her. That sort of thinking was believed, and even denounced, in the nineteenth century. The fact that it came out of the mouth of a white person in America claiming to be a Christian in the twenty-first century is appalling.

Finally, class and wealth have encouraged evangelicals to hold on to racism tightly as part of their beliefs about capitalism, God, and nation. It is why they have turned away from those who are impoverished and in need to support powerful businesses and politicians with money. By aligning themselves with both, their fortunes and ability to prosper have grown, and by engaging in capitalist enterprises themselves—for example, Chick-fil-A and Hobby Lobby are well known in this context—they have attained entrance to the country clubs and gated communities once out of their reach.

One need only to think about the Green family of Hobby Lobby, their staunch support of Republicans, and their building of the Museum of the Bible in Washington, D.C., as an example of religious capitalism used in the service of amassing political power and class status while being classified as a philanthropic organization. Recently, the sordid scandal involving Jerry Falwell Jr. and his wife, Becki, outlines what wealth, power, and proximity have done to evangelical leadership. Falwell, president of Liberty University, resigned after a sexual affair between his wife and Giancarlo Granda was revealed. Prior to the revelation, Falwell had tweeted a picture of a man, allegedly Virginia governor Ralph Northam, in blackface. Indiscreet sex (rather weakly depicted by Falwell as "cuckolding"), not racism, turns out to be a firing offense at Liberty University.

These in-your-face stories of evangelical leaders' failures may occasionally take the spotlight, but it is the deep-down racism embedded in evangelical beliefs, practices, and endeavors that truly requires believers to tell only a certain kind of story about themselves. Evangelicalism was important to furthering God's kingdom. Evangelicals fed the poor and the hungry. They brought the gospel to the far-flung reaches of the world and took care of the poor. Evangelicals opened colleges and universities and contributed to American life. Charismatic leaders asked the country to turn from its wicked ways and told us that abortion was the singular issue of our time. There is, however, this other story to tell.

Denominations verbally repented of racism but did little structurally to change it. Evangelicals promoted the family as one man and one woman, fought against gay rights, and lamented bitterly when same-sex marriage became the law of the land. Evangelicals disdained the Christian faith of the nation's first Black president. Evangelicals rejoiced when a thrice-married reality-TV-show star became president and called him King Cyrus, despite the fact that his administration imprisoned children on the borders, turned away refugees, and vilified fellow Black and Brown Americans. Evangelicals said little or nothing when he attacked people on Twitter or attacked women he did not like.

Access to power made evangelicalism brittle, and unforgiving. Ideology trumped the gospel. Loving your neighbor turned into loving only those who believe as you do. As a result, evangelicals live in silos to keep themselves pure. Theological, social, and cultural boundaries keep them from moving forward, leaving racially and ethnically different members with the cruel choice of having to deny their communities in order to be accepted or being kept on the fringes for "entertainment."

As a result, evangelicals are regarded with disdain by the broader public. Evangelicals wear this as a badge of honor and as a sign of persecution of

Christians. Evangelicals are not being persecuted in America. They are being called to *account*. Evangelicals are being judged for not keeping to the very morality they asked others to adhere to. They have been found wanting. Evangelicals comfort themselves in the arms of power, in symbols that Jesus disdained. They are the Pharisees.

Evangelicals capitulated. Evangelicals prevaricated. Evangelicals tolerated. Evangelicals participated. Jesus said, "By their fruits you shall know them." Evangelical fruit—the results of evangelicals' actions in civic life—today is rotten. Racism rotted it.

If this makes you nod your head and say yes, you can quit reading now. My work is done. But if you want to throw this book against the wall and you want to write me telling me you will pray for me (or something far worse), keep reading. This final section is for you.

What happens if evangelicals get everything they want? I've asked this question to my remaining evangelical friends who still talk to me and are open and willing to engage in a conversation about current politics and issues. In this case, getting everything you want for most evangelicals means overturning *Roe v. Wade*, building a conservative Supreme Court, creating a Christian nation (whatever that means), rescinding same-sex marriage, and somehow turning LGBTQ people into straights. A tall order.

None of these wishes, however, address racism. That's the biggest problem. It means that even when you get what you want, you can still be racist.

If you are an evangelical reading this book, then I would ask you to look around and see what your witness has wrought. The nation is polarized. The candidates you back want to take us back to a mythical time—apparently the 1950s—that honestly did not exist. The bile and hatred of some of the leaders you emulate make it impossible for people to believe whatever witness you have left. While you are clinging to God and guns, mothers are clinging to pictures of children who have been shot dead in classrooms, in streets, in malls, in cars. More people go hungry today than ever before. Inequality is mounting. Calls for law and order mean more Black and Brown bodies dead at the hands of the police. The nation's infrastructure is failing. Disdain for science has left America behind during a pandemic, while the rest of the world moves forward. The president you followed slavishly declared "American carnage" in his inaugural speech. Look around. You helped make this carnage we now experience.

All of these things have occurred because evangelicals, through religious lobbying and interference, supported the political structures that curtailed, limited, or struck down truly important issues. The polarization we are experiencing in government has stymied progress. That polarization has taken on a resemblance to ideological and theological battles. Your nationalistic evangelicalism is hurting others. Your racism is actively engaged in killing bodies and souls.

My analysis and prognostications may be dire, but it is never too late to make amends. Recent times have seen immense upheavals in American life—the horror of watching George Floyd's death for eight minutes and forty-six seconds, the vitality of Black Lives Matter marches, the surprisingly quick uprooting of Confederate statues, and an unrelenting stream of racist screeds from 1600 Pennsylvania Avenue. I watched with trepidation and a sliver of hope as evangelicals marched on a Sunday in Washington, D.C., in support of Black Lives Matter, with Senator Mitt Romney joining the group. North Central University, an Assemblies of God college in Minnesota, held the first funeral for George Floyd. Even Albert Mohler, former president of the Southern Baptist Convention, said, "The rise of Black Lives Matter points to the failure of the Christian Church to make the cause of human dignity and racial equality our own."

The sentiments are welcome. But there must be more. You must join with people you don't agree with in order to make a more perfect union, as the founders wanted. I am one of those people. I know you. I don't like the lies you've told yourself, and continue to tell to yourself and others, in order to try to hold on to power.

Ask yourself, What are you leaving as the posterity of American evangelicalism? What are the organizations you support leaving behind? Can you see past the individual sin of racism and understand that your votes, your choices, your actions participate in the structural support of white supremacy and racist policies and policing? Can you start to engage honestly and truthfully the actions of the leaders and politicians you support, to whom you have sold your souls for a mess of pottage? Can you step away from the headiness of being in the position of power to see the brokenness of your neighbors and the nation?

If you asked such questions, you would probably lose friends, and you might even lose your church home. Yes, I am asking a lot of you. To step out of the comfortable place you reside in while the world burns is difficult. It is, however, worth it. If you feel one ounce of conviction, then there is hope for you. There may even be hope for our nation.

I hope these words find root in you. I hope they trouble you. I hope they sear your soul. I hope they make you change. There is only a little time left, but there is time. The time is now.

ACKNOWLEDGMENTS

Books do not happen in a vacuum but in conversations, in camaraderie, and sometimes in despair. I've gone through all of these emotions in the writing of this book, but now it is time to give thanks.

I want to first thank Megan Carpentier, editor at NBC News THINK, for allowing me the latitude to write the op-ed that eventually led to this book. I am appreciative of your friendship and direction.

Thank you to Ruth Homrighaus at Ruthless Editing—I'm so glad we are back in touch, and thank you for your incisive edits and suggestions!

To Janice Rottenberg and Gabriel Raeburn, your love of religion and politics helped me to think through some of the important issues with this book. I'm very grateful to both of you for your enthusiasm, pointed questions, and research help.

Thanks as always to Sarah Posner, who, along with Peter Montgomery and members of the "posse" (you know who you are), has listened to me talk about this book and provided useful trajectories, as well as great cocktails! Thank you. I'll shut up now.

To my ride-or-die publicist, Tamika Franklin, ever ready to send over a video or article about evangelicals at 3 A.M. . . . keep on keeping on.

Thanks also to Yale Divinity School, which gave me the access I needed and space to work on not one but two books as a Presidential Fellow in 2019–20.

I am pleased to acknowledge the support of the funders who created the Marcie Cohen Ferris and William R. Ferris Imprint at UNC Press.

Most of all, a special, heartfelt thank-you to Elaine Maisner, executive editor at UNC Press, who has been solidly in my corner as an advocate, friend, and editor. You helped me finish this book after my illness during the COVID-19 pandemic. You believed in me, and I'm eternally grateful for your support and friendship.

SELECTED READING

1850–1930

Baker, Kelly J. *The Gospel According to the Klan: The KKK's Appeal to Protestant America, 1915–1930*. Lawrence: University of Kansas Press, 2011.

Gloege, Timothy. *Guaranteed Pure: The Moody Bible Institute, Business, and the Making of Modern Evangelicalism*. Chapel Hill: University of North Carolina Press, 2015.

Haynes, Stephen R. *Noah's Curse: The Biblical Justification for American Slavery*. New York: Oxford University Press, 2002.

Mathews, Donald G. *At the Altar of Lynching: Burning Sam Hose in the American South*. New York: Cambridge University Press, 2017.

Ribuffo, Leo. *The Old Christian Right: The Protestant Far Right from the Great Depression to the Cold War*. Philadelphia: Temple University Press, 1983.

Sutton, Matthew Avery. *American Apocalypse: A History of Modern Evangelicalism*. Cambridge, Mass.: Belknap, 2014.

Wilson, Charles Reagan. *Baptized in Blood: The Religion of the Lost Cause, 1865–1920*. Athens: University of Georgia Press, 2009.

1942–1967

Dochuk, Darren. *From Bible Belt to Sunbelt: Plain-Folk, Religion, Grassroots Politics, and the Rise of Evangelical Conservatism*. New York: W. W. Norton, 2011.

Dupont, Carolyn Renée. *Mississippi Praying: Southern White Evangelicals and the Civil Rights Movement, 1945–1975*. New York: New York University Press, 2013.

Hendershot, Heather. *What's Fair in the Air? Cold War Right-Wing Broadcasting and the Public Interest*. Chicago: University of Chicago Press, 2011.

Kruse, Kevin M. *One Nation under God: How Corporate America Invented Christian America*. New York: Basic Books, 2015.

Marsden, George M. *Reforming Fundamentalism: Fuller Seminary and the New Evangelicalism*. Grand Rapids, Mich.: W. B. Eerdmans, 1995.

Martin, William. *With God on Our Side: The Rise of the Religious Right in America*. New York: Broadway Books, 1996.

McGirr, Lisa. *Suburban Warriors: The Origins of the New American Right*. Princeton, N.J.: Princeton University Press, 2001.

Miller, Steven P. *Billy Graham and the Rise of the Republican South*. Philadelphia: University of Pennsylvania Press, 2009.

Williams, Daniel K. *God's Own Party: The Making of the Christian Right*. New York: Oxford University Press, 2010.

1968–2000

Balmer, Randall. "The Real Origins of the Religious Right." *Politico*, May 27, 2014. www.politico.com/magazine/story/2014/05/religious-right-real-origins-107133.

Crespino, Joseph. "Civil Rights and the Religious Right." In *Rightward Bound: Making American Conservatism in the 1970s*, edited by Bruce J. Shulman and Julian E. Zelizer, 90–105. Cambridge, Mass.: Harvard University Press, 2008.

Critchlow, Donald. *Phyllis Schlafly and Grassroots Conservatism: A Woman's Crusade*. Princeton, N.J.: Princeton University Press, 2005.

Dowland, Seth. *Family Values and the Rise of the Christian Right*. Philadelphia: University of Pennsylvania Press, 2015.

Griffith, R. Marie. *Moral Combat: How Sex Divided American Christians and Fractured American Politics*. New York: Basic Books, 2017.

Hartman, Andrew. *A War for the Soul of America: A History of the Culture Wars*. Chicago: University of Chicago Press, 2015.

Hunter, James Davison. *Culture Wars: The Struggle to Define America*. New York: Basic Books, 1991.

Johnson, Emily S. *This Is Our Message: Women's Leadership in the New Christian Right*. New York: Oxford University Press, 2019.

Moreton, Bethany. *To Serve God and Wal-Mart: The Making of Christian Free Enterprise*. Cambridge, Mass.: Harvard University Press, 2010.

2000–2020

Butler, Anthea. "From Republican Party to Republican Religion: The New Political Evangelists of the Right." *Political Theology* 13, no. 5 (2012): 634–51.

Du Mez, Kristin Kobes. *Jesus and John Wayne: How White Evangelicals Corrupted a Faith and Fractured the Nation.* New York: Liveright, 2020.

Emerson, Michael O., and Christian Smith. *Divided by Faith: Evangelical Religion and the Problem of Race in America.* New York: Oxford University Press, 2000.

Hughey, Matthew W. *The Wrongs of the Right: Language, Race, and the Republican Party in the Age of Obama.* New York: New York University Press, 2014.

Marti, Geraldo. *American Blindspot: Race, Class, Religion, and the Trump Presidency.* Lanham, Md.: Rowman and Littlefield, 2020.

Posner, Sarah. *God's Profits: Faith, Fraud, and the Republican Crusade for Values Voters.* Sausalito, Calif.: Polipoint, 2008.

———. *Unholy: Why White Evangelicals Worship at the Altar of Donald Trump.* New York: Random House, 2020.

Sharlet, Jeff. *The Family: The Secret Fundamentalism at The Heart of American Power.* New York: HarperCollins, 2008.

Whitehead, Andrew L., and Samuel L. Perry. *Taking America Back for God: Christian Nationalism in the United States.* New York: Oxford University Press, 2020.

INDEX